SUCCESSFUL
CHURCH FUND-RAISING

CAPITAL CAMPAIGNS
YOU CAN DO YOURSELF

JOHN R. BISAGNO
PASTOR EMERITUS, FIRST BAPTIST CHURCH, HOUSTON

BROADMAN
&HOLMAN
PUBLISHERS

NASHVILLE, TENNESSEE

0–8054–2495–4

Published by Broadman & Holman Publishers, Nashville, Tennessee

Subject Heading: FUND-RAISING

Old Testament Scripture quotations are from the Holy Bible, New International Version, copyright © 1973, 1978, 1984 by International Bible Society. New Testament Scripture quotations are from the Holman Christian Standard Bible, © 2000 by Holman Bible Publishers. Used by Permission.

2 3 4 5 6 7 8 9 10 06 05 04 03 02

To my son-in-law, Dr. Curt Dodd,

whose expertise and excellence

in Christian financial stewardship

and truly great affection

for Christ and his church

helped develop these concepts

across many faithful years of ministry.

CONTENTS

FOREWORD

WEBSTER'S NEW COLLEGIATE DICTIONARY offers several rather impressive definitions of *hero:* "a mythological or legendary figure often of divine descent endowed with great strength or ability; a man admired for his achievements and qualities."

Far from mythological but definitely a child of the King, Dr. John Bisagno fits the definitions and qualifies as one of my heroes. Though not a member of his church or his denomination, I grew up in Houston and watched from a distance as he led First Baptist Church in relocating and developing one of the finest church campuses in America. I observed the impact his ministry had on the fourth largest city in the United States and marveled at the effectiveness of their outreach. I read his books, listened to his tapes, even heard him in person a few times. And I was always amazed at his passion, especially for the local church and for the shepherds of these flocks, small and large, across denominational lines.

Somewhere along my pastoral journey I heard a rumor that this megachurch pastor everyone called "Brother John" had a heart for young pastors trying to find their way in ministry. I understood that he would demonstrate that love with some of his time. So when our paths providentially crossed, I decided to take a chance and see if the rumors were true. I attended a board meeting of a proposed Christian high school. Dr. Bisagno was spearheading this multimillion-dollar project, which is now Houston Christian High School. I asked if he would allow me to tag along sometime when he was making a short trip for a speaking engagement. He graciously consented, and I began to make a mental list of the hundreds of ministry questions I had in mind for him to answer.

A few weeks later his secretary called my office, and arrangements were made for me to accompany Brother John on a trip to a small town in East Texas where he would speak to several hundred people about the power of prayer. It was during the course of the evening that I related our local church's need to build another building, our second in three years. My greatest concern was fund-raising; we were in the final days of receiving pledges from the last capital stewardship campaign, and the expense of another campaign, dealing with fund-raising companies and trying to keep all the work of ministry going had about as much appeal as trying to change a tire on a moving automobile.

My discouragement quickly disappeared as my new friend began to tell me how we could conduct the campaign ourselves and save thousands of dollars in the process. Over the course of the next few weeks, much of the information contained in this very helpful and practical book was developed and implemented. Dr. Bisagno's wisdom and expertise in understanding the principles of motivating and mobilizing a congregation were right on target. Several months later we celebrated the most successful capital stewardship campaign in the history of the church. A new building was completed while the congregation continued to grow in all categories. Leaders were developed for future ministries, and faith was strengthened and matured as a result of engaging in this capital stewardship program.

Since that time I have seen and helped other churches, large and small, follow this step-by-step procedure for planning, organizing, and implementing a capital stewardship plan directed by the lay leadership of a local congregation. Each time the goals have been met, and the congregation has been strengthened through the process.

I'm convinced the problem is never a lack of resources, only a lack of vision. Cast the vision with a passion and resources will flow to see that vision become a reality. Bill Gates, CEO of Microsoft, once said, "It's pretty hard to be successful if all you're doing is thinking about some business goal. It's a lot easier if you pick something you bring a passion to."

Spend some time with my mentor and friend, Brother John, and you will discover his enthusiasm and passion for the ministry of the local church and its pastors. Spend some time with this book, and you will find a plan that engages your church to passionately pursue their dreams.

Keith Newman, Senior Pastor
Mission Valley Church of the Nazarene
San Diego, California

INTRODUCTION

UNDER THE MANDATE OF THE GREAT COMMISSION, no evangelical church can even consider losing pace or momentum. It is ever onward and upward, reaching, expanding, and growing for the followers of Christ. That means new buildings, and new buildings mean new money.

The men and women who serve as professional fund-raisers helping churches raise capital funds, particularly in the realm of land acquisition and building programs, are some of God's great gifts to the church. Generally speaking, these professionals do an excellent job of helping churches raise new capital to meet the ever-expanding building program needs of a growing church, and are often worth the money. But every great growing church was once a small church, which could ill afford the tens and even hundreds of thousands of dollars these professionals charge. And yet for these churches and for the kingdom, the expansion of their facilities is just as important as it is for the larger churches. The expertise of the professional fund-raiser is probably economically out of reach for at least 95 percent of the millions of churches in the world, and it is to these churches that I offer my assistance.

THE JOY OF GIVING TO THE KINGDOM

IN 1966, IT WAS MY PRIVILEGE to help revise the first handbook on professional Christian fund-raising. From that moment, I have never been far away from the grass roots of the fund-raising ministry. I have helped churches organize to raise money, and I have spoken at uncountable pledge banquets and consulted with pastors, all the while leading my own congregation—our beloved First Baptist Church of Houston—to give about $250 million from 1970 to 2000 to budgets, buildings, and missions.

Additionally, God has given me the acquaintance and lifelong friendship of some of the finest fund-raisers in America. By experience, by conversation, and by observation, I have had the opportunity to learn the business inside out. But perhaps even more than all this, I am compelled to write this book because, frankly, I love to raise money for the cause of Christ and to help others do so as well. This will sound foreign to the ears of many pastors, because I find the mention of money to one's congregation to be perhaps the single most difficult part of the ministry for most pastors.

Let me say again, I love it. I really do. There are, I think, two reasons why this is true: One, I love to see the kingdom of God grow. Ours has always been an unselfish church and ministry. Here in First Baptist, Houston, we believe that the kingdom of God is first, and our own church is second. I have the joy of pastoring the most unselfish congregation on the globe. Our people give themselves away in money, in time, and in service. Every Sunday I give two invitations: one to join the church and one to leave the church. I love to send our people out to serve. The lovely young Christian woman who is at this moment typing these words just shared with me the joy of her personal involvement with one of our local missions. We have sent millions of dollars and hundreds of our people, not only to the distant foreign mission fields of the world, but to the remote corners of our own city's scores of ethnic mission opportunities. On any given Sunday, nearly as many persons worship the Lord and find him as Savior through our mission ministries in Houston as in the home facilities of our own local congregation.

There's no greater joy than living with a kingdom mind-set, and I love to help expand the kingdom of God. The Holy Spirit certainly made no mistake when he birthed the church on the day of Pentecost. He knew we would need one another. And not only do we need one another other within our own local congregations, but we need one another within the larger kingdom, in other churches and other denominations, in other places, in other cities, and in other states and lands. As you think through what you are reading, I am breathing a little prayer in my heart that God will expand your horizons and give you a kingdom mind-set as well.

Christianity is about a cross, and a cross is "I" crossed out. Jesus said, "For whoever wants to save his life will lose it, but whoever loses his life because of Me and the gospel will save it" (Mark 8:35). To the veracity and validity of that promise, I attest by my own personal experience, with glad joy and great faith.

Give, give to others. Help others; give away your time, money, talents, resources, expertise, and gifts. If you're giving for the kingdom of God, it's good. Jesus' great priority was that the kingdom of God would come on earth and his will be done on earth as both his kingdom and his will exist in heaven.

At this writing, I am involved in helping raise funds for First Baptist Church, Houston; Spring Baptist Church, Spring, Texas; First Church of the Nazarene, Houston; International Mission Board of the Southern Baptist Convention; a prison administered by Christians in Sugar Land, Texas; the ministry of Jeanette Cliff George's After Dinner Players; First Baptist Academy; Houston Christian High School; a city-wide crusade in Asheville, North Carolina; Falls Creek Assembly; Southwestern Baptist Seminary in Fort Worth; and an educational center which will honor, among others, Dr. Harry Piland, former minister of education at First Baptist Church, Houston.

People ask me, "Why are you not protective of your congregation? Why do you not try to insulate them against other fund-raisers who are trying to get the same money from them for their causes that you are for yours?" The answer is simple. I don't have a selfish heart. I am for the kingdom. If it's for God's glory, the honor of Christ, and the souls of men, I'm for it and I'll support it. First Baptist Church of Houston will not win everybody in Houston, let alone the world, to Christ. We need one another, we need to help one another, and we need to support one another. And I find no greater fulfillment in my life than doing that.

You do not hurt your own ministry when you help other ministries. In teaching your people to be generous with other causes, they will be generous with your cause. In learning to open their hearts to the Lord, to give in one place, they will be more generous in giving every place. And, remember, *you don't have to protect people's pocketbooks*. They will do that very well for themselves, thank you. The problem is not that we have to protect them from giving more than they should, more than they can, or more than the Lord wants them to; the problem is to protect them against giving less than they should, less than they can, and less than our Father would have them give.

Giving is a joy. Giving is a delight. You cannot outgive God. Remember the promise of Luke 6:38: "Give, and it will be given to you; a good measure, pressed down, shaken together, and running over will be poured into your lap. For with the measure that you use, it will be measured back to you." So I can honestly say that I give, and I enjoy inspiring and teaching people to give because I love it. And I'm praying right now that you, as pastors and church leaders reading this book, will learn to love it too. Don't apologize. Lead your people to give and give generously.

But there's a second reason I love to help people learn to give. Not only do I love the process and love to see the kingdom grow, but I love it because I know when I teach people to give, I do them a tremendous favor. I believe the greatest thing I can do for people is to lead them to faith in Jesus Christ. The second greatest thing is to teach them how to walk in the power of the Holy Spirit. And the third best thing I can do is to teach them how to be rightly related to God in their finances.

Dear pastor, hear me. When you teach people to give and lead them to give sacrificially, joyously, abundantly, and gregariously, you're not hurting them. You're helping them, and doing them a great favor. As they learn to give, the Father will increasingly give back to each of them. So pray that God will give you a heart for giving and a heart for the joy of leading your people to give. Nothing will be more important than your positive attitude as you lead your congregation through the steps of the fund-raising program for your capital needs that I outline in this book.

Remember, three things are important: *attitude, attitude, attitude*. Be positive, be joyous, and don't apologize. You can do it. The resources are there and the need is great. On a recent Sunday morning, I shared with our congregation that we were about $300,000 short on the funding of our new Christian grade school. I said it like this: "Well, church, today I've got some bad news, some good news and some bad news. The bad news is we're about $300,000 behind on our giving to the building fund. The good news is, however, that God has abundantly provided, and we have the money. The bad news is, it's in your pockets." Of course, everyone laughed, but there's more truth than humor in my announcement. God owns the cattle on a thousand hills. His people control trillions of dollars of God's capital. It's there, and we can access it. The key is to explain to the people the need, present a logical, reasonable, thought-out plan to meet the need, inspire them to meet it, and give them the opportunity.

For over a third of a century of pastoring churches, I have lived by this philosophy: *God's people, given the facts, will normally do the right thing.* Tell the Lord, tell the folks, be positive, be joyous, and above all, remember that your positive attitude is critical. Don't apologize. You're not just expanding the kingdom; you're helping the people as well. Fund-raising builds the kingdom and blesses the folks. Don't be fearful and don't be negative. Positively, joyously, abundantly, and expectantly, go to the Lord and go to your people, and watch what God will do.

2

YOU CAN BE YOUR OWN FUND-RAISER

I OFTEN HEAR THE COMMENT, "If only I had a big church with lots of workers and lots of money, my ministry would be easier." Let me assure you that large churches have precisely the same needs that small churches do. If you're a thousand dollars behind on your budget, that large church down the street is probably a hundred thousand behind on its budget. If you're struggling to enlist three new workers in your Sunday school, they are probably scrambling to find fifty-three. My point is simple: No matter how many zeros you add behind the equation, the concepts are constant and the principles consistent.

Accordingly, what you find in this book will work in any church, large or small. Regardless of how many members you have and how much you're trying to raise, the principles are constant. What I'm going to share with you will work anywhere, in any size congregation. We're going to examine how to determine what you really need before we even think about how to raise the money to do it. Because if the need is not sound, reasonable, well thought-out, logical, and sellable, the whole program is built on a flawed premise, and you will not be successful. Before you even begin to think about whether to build, how much it will cost, and how to raise it, there are some important steps to take.

Most capital campaigns for "over-and-above" funds beyond weekly budget giving center on a three-year pledge. We're going to look at a formula for determining how much the people can reasonably be expected to pledge above their present level of giving, factoring in, of course, your potential for future growth during the three-year pledge period. It is imperative that the amount you determine is reasonable to pledge and that it matches the cost of what you are planning to do. The possibility exists that while you can only reasonably expect to raise $600,000, you want to enter a $2 million building program. Don't even think about it. The gap is too wide, the reach too far.

Reason and faith must come together here. What God intends you to acquire in land or buildings as your next step will and must coincide with the provision he has placed within the resources of your people to fund it. If they can only reasonably give $600,000 above the present level of budget giving over the next three years, don't challenge them to give $2 million. Seven hundred thousand, maybe, perhaps even $800,000 or $900,000, but a reach too far will ensure failure and will be counterproductive to future campaigns.

But the good news is, if $600,000 is all the Lord has provided within the resources of his people, then $600,000 is all the next step should be. The key, then, is to determine what is the right next intermediate step, rather than what may be the ultimate visionary dream step which you may be unreasonably and unrealistically attempting to take at this time.

So let's start with determining what is the right next step, with the confident assurance that, though it may not be precisely what you had envisioned or would like to take, it will be the right step, because where God leads, God provides, and the right step will match with the right resources. When God is in it, both will come together, eliminating the reach too far. That way there will be success, the people will be encouraged, and you will be in a position to embark upon a second campaign at some point. It is imperative that the people have a good experience, and a reasonable goal for a reasonable next step is a part of the recipe for that to happen.

Unfortunately, some overanxious fund-raisers lead churches to believe they can do more than they can and get the people all excited when, in fact, no sound thinking has gone into what the church can reasonably do. So before we talk about the formula to determine what your church can realistically commit, let's talk about the logical next step: the project itself to which you are asking your people to pledge.

3

A TIME TO BUILD

GOD HAS PUT IT IN THE HEART OF HIS PEOPLE to expand themselves, expand his glory, and expand his kingdom. We are by nature a gregarious, going, giving, and reaching people as the children of God. The Datsun Motor Company, now the Nissan Company, used to have a fantastic advertising slogan. It said it simply but said it well, not only for them but also for us: "We are driven." As God's kids, we, too, are a driven people. We are driven to the end of ourselves by the love of Christ. We are driven to the ends of the earth by the Great Commission. We are driven to the end of time by the imminent coming of our Savior. There is always that holy compulsion for more—more souls, more ministry, more service, more giving—and we have to have the buildings in which to minister and the land on which to place the buildings. So there will always be that holy "drivenness" about the church of Jesus Christ. We can, we must, and we will never let up. As long as one soul remains unsaved, one nation unreached, one land unclaimed for Christ, the divine obsession must never die. Remember, Jesus builds the church, but we must build the church buildings.

The satisfied church is the church doomed to die. Deep in the chests of the leaders of the congregation, along with that of the pastor, beat driven hearts, but unfortunately, the challenge of finding funds to fight the battle drives them as well. "If only we had the money. How can we raise the money, buy the land, and build the building, so that our ministries can go forward?" It is not a chicken-and-egg question. It is not a merry-go-round without a beginning. There is a starting point, and the starting point is determining the right next step in the process. What is the reasonable next move forward? Remember, Rome wasn't built in a day, and it is seldom, if ever, within the wise and perfect will of God to do it all at once. Slow, steady growth is much more desirable than booming overnight growth.

As you are building buildings, you must be building people, building stewardship, and building faith. A building too heavy on the top and too light on the foundation is destined to fall. The strongest part of the building must be the first layer, the foundation. So, do not try to get there all at once. Let us not think about a three-thousand-seat sanctuary, education space for twenty-five hundred, offices, gymnasiums and parking lots all at once. Let us think about a logical and reasonable sequence, bite-sized and tailor-made to both reality and resources.

Before we move forward, let's back up a step further and answer this: Are you absolutely certain the next step is the building or land acquisition at all? It may be that you do not need a capital campaign. Perhaps the next stretching of the people's resources should be an investment in personnel or television or missions or Sunday school materials. The balancing of buildings, staff, missions, and program money in a church budget is very important.

Nothing will be of any greater value in this book than to get hold of this truth: People are your greatest resource, and people never transcend their leadership. The number one priority in your church budget should be quality staff. A pastor whose staff consists only of a combination music, youth, and education director plus a part-time secretary is not even close to thinking about a million-dollar building project. Your primary budget must go to quality staff first, and then to buildings and missions. Without a staff to lead the church, the people will never be able to do much in missions or buildings or stewardship.

Presumably, you bought this book because you want to raise money, whether thousands or millions, to buy land and/or to build buildings. That proposition presupposes that you are actually growing and in need of those buildings. If you're not growing, then let's think about some other things that may be more important than buildings. If you are not currently growing because membership has boomed and you are now out of space, then read on. But if you are not growing because there is division in the church, the staff is weak, the pastor is not being followed or other negative factors, then you need to address different issues before you think about raising money for new buildings.

New buildings will not attract people. People come to church because there's a loving, warm, bright, positive, empathetic, encouraging atmosphere, and where they feel deeply in their heart that the pastor and people love them, care about them, and truly accept them as they are. Let me say that again. Churches try to build from two positions: strength and weakness. If you are building from a position of strength because you are doing so well and have to build to keep growing, then build. But if you are building because no one is coming and you think new buildings will attract new people, you will be sadly disappointed.

People today have virtually no commitment to institutions or tradition. They do not go to a church primarily because of its doctrine or its denomination. The facts that Daddy was a Methodist and Granddaddy was a Methodist have little to do with today's people deciding to be Methodist.

People select a church for these reasons:

1. There is a great spirit. It is loving, friendly, positive, upbeat, and accepting. Look around you. The landscape is dotted with thousands of gothic, magnificent, cathedral-like edifices that are empty on the inside, while down the street, churches in storefronts and broken-down buildings are packing them in with the love of Jesus. The spirit and quality of a church are vastly more important than its buildings.
2. The preaching is biblical, easily understandable, and applicable to my life and my needs.
3. The music speaks to my heart; it is exciting, moving, and joyous.
4. There are people there who are like me. I feel comfortable around those with whom I worship.
5. There are good programs for my family, especially my teenagers and my children. Regardless of its unsound doctrine, even bordering on heresy, people will leave your church and go down the street to "Brand X Church" because the nurseries are attractive, secure, and well run. And quality programs, relevant preaching, and great atmosphere begin with good leadership.
6. The facilities offer good, well-paved, accessible parking.

In summary, you may need to think about a major investment in two or three good additional staff members before you think about new buildings. A word to the wise here: One outstanding staff member is of more value than three average or pretty good staff members, and you must expect to pay more for that exceptional person. I would much more readily pay a $100,000 salary for the finest staff member in America in his or her field than have three $33,000 staff members who are just adequate. Saving money on staff is counterproductive. Perhaps your next step is to upgrade your staff. Investment in people is always a priority investment for a successful church.

Another thing to consider before you make the decision to build is the use of existing space. Are you utilizing what you already have to the maximum? Perhaps a new sign, a new coat of paint, some pretty shrubbery and flowers, along with brightening up the spirit of what's happening inside those walls and beginning dual services would be better next steps.

It is always wise to give serious consideration to using one building twice before you think about building a new building twice as large and using it once. There is not only the wisdom of the economy of such a decision, but the attractiveness of more than one service time to the community. Remember this about today's society: People like choices. Let me put it even more strongly: People demand choices!

At our church in Houston, we offer various types of ministries, many different entry points into the church, and various kinds of worship services and music with varied schedules. The apostle Paul reminded us, "I have become all things to all people, so that I may by all means save some" (1 Cor. 9:22b). Not everyone will be reached by the same means. We have many "side door entrances" into our church. One may be a counseling ministry or a youth group. Another may be an aerobics class or a support group, or any one of an uncountable number of other entry points. But because they have various choices, thousands of worshipers make our church their choice each Sunday of the year.

Do not ever even think about compromising the gospel. No! The message must never change, but the methods must be ever changing. What is your church doing about that "all things" portion of Paul's admonition?

Every study of the Boomers, the X-ers, the Busters, and all the rest of us indicate that people want choices. Not choices in doctrine, not choices about the road to heaven, but choices in programming and scheduling, and today's church must provide them. None is more glaringly obvious than the offering of different services at different times. Currently, we offer four Sunday options: 8:15, 9:30, and 11:00 A.M., and 6:30 P.M. As recently as this week, we have had serious dialogue with our church leadership exploring yet other options. The Youth for Christ folks have a wonderful slogan, "Geared to the times, but anchored to the Rock." I like that. Stay anchored to the Rock, but stay in tune with the times, and the times are telling you that people want options.

One of the best options is two morning worship services and two Bible study times. If I were a layman, I would attend the earliest service you offered me in order that I might have more time with my family through the day. Many people prefer an early worship hour while others prefer to sleep late and come to late worship. Don't try to fit everyone into the same cookie-cutter mold. Give them the options they hunger for. So, before you make plans to build a bigger building for one congregation, seriously consider whether you should put two different congregations in the one building you already have. Many varying models exist. There is, of course, the flip-flop where one group goes to Sunday school at 9:00 and church at 10:30, while another group goes to church at 9:00 and then Sunday school at 10:30. One of the advantages is that a choice of options is offered with many variations on the basic theme. One of the potential disadvantages is the temptation for parents to go to church, only to church, while their children attend only Sunday school at the same time, and both go home, investing only one hour on Sunday morning. Unfortunately, in this scenario, the parents never get to Bible study, and the children never get to worship. But this can usually be offset by constantly reminding the parents of the importance of bringing their children to worship and of being in Bible study.

Another nice variation of dual services is the staggered schedule. Group A goes to Sunday school at 8:30 and worship at 9:45. Group B goes to Sunday school at 9:45 and worship at 11:00. There are three advantages here. One, the order is sequential. Everybody goes to Sunday school first and then to church. Two, it is simple and easy to understand. You simply choose Schedule A, 8:15 and 9:45; or, Schedule B, 9:45 and 11:00. Three, traffic and parking patterns offer less congestion, with better ingress and egress. Obviously, churches with too little Sunday school space and too much worship space can have one worship service in the middle with dual Sunday schools on either side. In the opposite scenario, one great central Sunday school can be bracketed by worship services before and after. Virtually any minister of education at a large and growing church could consult with you about other pros, cons, and varying models, but the flip-flop and the staggered schedule are two good, basic options as you address the issue, "Is the next step to build more buildings or to use the ones we have more effectively?"

As you make these decisions, remember their relative importance to parking, which is monumental. One of the things that will help you is to determine a reasonable, Holy Spirit-led goal toward which your church could and should grow over the next ten to fifteen years. We would all like to have ten thousand, but there may be in your future a reasonable stopping point of five hundred, a thousand or two thousand, at which you start to grow on off-campus locations. Missions, outreach centers, and Bible studies can, as we have said, expand the kingdom of God beyond the property on which your church buildings are located. Explore the mind of Christ in this area.

Nearly three thousand people worship every Sunday in the mission churches we have started here in Houston. They're part of the kingdom and of the umbrella of our church, but to physically add those numbers to our existing home base would be logistically impossible. In addition, the needs of those varying groups are often much better served in the mission church model.

Prayerfully consider the price of the land and buildings, the economic capabilities of your people (using the formula which we shall shortly explore) and the mind of Christ, as the Spirit of God leads you to a comprehensive, long-range plan for your church.

Once you have determined what that number is on your home base location, the maximum number of people you can reach, and the buildings you will build with the service schedule you determine, then you must answer these three questions:

1. How many parking spaces are necessary for the cars that will bring those people on Sunday morning (the maximum number that will be there at any given time)?
2. How many people will be in those cars and how many can be parked per acre?
3. How many acres will we need to park those cars, in addition to the other facilities, recreation ministry, fellowship center, kitchen, Sunday school space, worship center, rest rooms, landscaping, driveways, and other space requirements?

Over the next six Sundays, keep statistics to answer these two questions:

1. What is the maximum number of people who are on our property and in our buildings at the peak attendance time on Sunday morning?
2. How many cars are parked in the parking lot?

The formula is easy. If attendance is six hundred people and you count two hundred cars, they are coming three to a car. Include babies and children in your count. Our church attracts many singles, and we know our average to be between 2.2 and 2.3 persons per car. When you figure the number of cars you can park per acre, you must factor in entrances, exits, and driveways. The latest and best figure, including the above factors, is about 110 cars per acre. Do the percentages in your parking lot on how many big cars are coming as opposed to how many compact cars, and presume that the number of smaller cars may increase slightly but gradually through the years. If you expect to realistically reach a thousand people per Sunday long-range and God has led you to that assumption, then figure how many acres you will require to park the cars using the above formula. Add in the space you will need for worship center, education, recreation, supporting and all other facilities, and that is the amount of land you need to own.

Keep two things in mind: You can usually secure adjoining land by paying a small amount for an option to buy the land in the future without actually paying the full amount to purchase the land today, and you can never have too much land. Many churches have been blessed by buying a large parcel of land and being able to sell off part of it through the years to pay for the rest of it. I do not suggest that you do this unless God specifically leads you because I do not think he particularly intends for his churches to be in the investment real estate business. But just tuck the thought away in the back of your mind that this could be a possibility in the future.

Far better too much land than too little. And I speak from experience. We are landlocked. We greatly underestimated our potential and the space we would need. Today fourteen policemen direct the traffic on Sundays, and seven or eight shuttle buses take the people to several distant parking lots. We greatly need to invest in more space and more land, but there is one problem. We did not buy enough land when we first relocated; and by the time we realized we needed it, the cost was a million dollars an acre, and we decided a purchase at that price was not feasible. Today, others have bought the land, and now surround us. I have spoken with hundreds of pastors through the years who are landlocked and struggling with the issue of relocation because the church was originally built on only five or six acres. I have never known a pastor, however, struggling with the problem of too much land. There is no such thing as a church having too much land.

4

DETERMINING THE SUCCESS
OF YOUR CAMPAIGN

SEVERAL FACTORS GO INTO DETERMINING the feasibility of a fund-raiser to take the church to the next level in the realization of new space. The first and perhaps most important is this: Do the people really love the Lord and love lost souls? Is there a passion, not just for this building program, but also for the work of Christ and the expansion of his kingdom? Satan is at work in the kingdom. What God sows, Satan oversows. What God plants, Satan often pulls up. And nowhere has he greater expertise than in this area. Satan loves to keep God's people unsettled.

There is always an unspoken, often even unrecognized, tension in the heart of God's people between the compelling constraints of the Great Commission and the feeling that we really are pretty well satisfied with the way things are. All those new people mean new leadership. There may be more of them than there are of us before long. We may lose our control. Will they take over? Will they change things? There is a lot of security in the status quo, but the seeds of death are there as well. The church that is not moving forward is not standing still it is moving backwards. And the church that is moving in reverse is doomed to die.

Your people have to come to grips with this question: Are we really willing to risk losing our control, our positions, and the security that lies in keeping things as they are for the sake of reaching an unsaved world? It is a question too many congregations have faced, and made the wrong choice.

The first factor in determining the feasibility of a campaign to expand facilities is to ask this question: Are the people willing to commit to a cause greater than their own security and even their very identity? New buildings mean new people. New people mean change, and change can be unsettling.

Second, do the people love the pastor? Do they rally around him as God's special undershepherd, believe in him, support him, and follow him? Leadership in a church is a delicate thing. It must be earned and not demanded, deserved and not coerced. Yet it must be granted by a mature congregation which recognizes at once the frailties of human leadership and the holiness of the office to which God has called the undershepherd. A pastor on shaky ground with his people is not a good candidate to lead a major campaign for a building program. If they have not followed him in the little things, they will likely not follow him in this big thing.

It was in the heart of David to build a temple for God, and building the temple was within God's will. But neither the timing nor the circumstances were right for David. God did accomplish that which he put in David's heart, but the temple was built in another day and at another time, not by King David, but by King Solomon, his son. It may well be that as pastor, you have the right plan but do not have the right time. Perhaps another will finish what you begin, and that is all right as long as we truly believe that the end result is all for God's glory and none of ours.

Third, have you taken your leadership with you? Have those in whom the church has confidence been involved in the decision-making process as you have patiently and methodically studied the ingredients of this decision and come with confidence to say, "This is what we believe God would have us do?" Pastor, do not stand alone. There is wisdom in many counselors, and you must take your leadership with you as you gently lead them through the process of determining the rationale and the feasibility of the building program you are about to recommend to your people. Do not get in a hurry. Make sure everyone is on board, anticipate all the questions that may arise, and be prepared to give reasonable and thoughtful answers to your people.

Fourth, do the people clearly understand the facts? Take the time to thoroughly inform them about the decision you are recommending. Help them to understand the process that you have completed, including what the program will produce, what it will provide and for whom, what it will accomplish, what it will cost, and how the church will pay for it. Explain the processes for naming the building committee, interviewing architects, employing a contractor, and other items important to your congregation. Remember, God's people will indeed make the right decision when you have given them all the facts.

Once you have done that, do not rush them to a decision. Present the information, and have a couple of meetings with questions and answers in which the steering committee stands beside you and shares in answering all the questions. You, as pastor, will have built up to this time by preaching inspiring sermons about the importance of expanding the kingdom. It is important to inform the people and bring them along with you step-by-step. Informed people are happy people.

Fifth, is there a spirit of unity, happiness, and joy in the church? Are the people excited not only about their pastor and about reaching souls, but are they excited about the Lord and about one another? Do they feel good about the church? A church in division and disarray is not ready to enter a building program.

There are two primary areas of consideration that go into determining the feasibility of your program. There are the hard-core ingredients of the economics of your people; that is to say, how much can they potentially pledge and give if they do so at the maximum? But what they *can* do must be measured against what they *will* do, and what they will do is determined by the five factors above, which comprise the spiritual and emotional ingredients of the program.

If any of the above is lacking, there will be a negative impact on what the people pledge to the campaign. You might not be the right person to lead in regard to expansion building at this time. It may indeed be a David and Solomon situation or maybe you are the right leader, but the timing is wrong. Perhaps the church needs a period of lay renewal. Perhaps the body needs to understand more the imperative of the Great Commission, the importance of Christian unity, and the significance of the office of pastor. Perhaps you need to delay the program as you work on these areas, for when they are operating at maximum potential, the people will go much further in what they *will* do in relationship to what they *can* do.

5

HOW MUCH WILL THE PEOPLE PLEDGE?

LET'S ASSUME THAT ALL THE FACTORS ARE IN PLACE, and everything is coming up roses. You've considered parking, staff, multiple services, land acquisition, building costs, willingness to stretch and change, love for the pastor, confidence in the pastor, desire to grow, and love for the Lord and one another, and all systems are "go." Your people want to reach people. You and your team have explained the need to them, and they see the need, are willing to meet the need, and have confidence in their leaders to lead them through the process.

Now comes the moment of truth. All the above being optimal, how much are your people realistically capable of pledging over three years?

First, let us clear away some underbrush. If you have a reasonable need, a sound program, a firm financial history, and a stable congregation, most banks will lend you the money to enter the building program. I strongly urge you not to wait three years until the money is in the bank until you hire an architect, get the bids, and begin construction. Waiting is counterproductive for two reasons: First, potential enthusiasm and time are lost, and the people may become disheartened with the stagnation of delay; and second, inflation will hurt you, for the building will cost more in three years than it will today. The sooner you build, the less expensive it will be. It does not make sense to delay. When nothing is going on, the people are not excited. When they see the building going up, they tend to give more. You will not receive contributions to the program as fast if you are waiting three years to build.

If you are building a million-dollar facility, during the actual construction the congregation will likely give $700,000 or $800,000. If no construction is going on during the same one- or two-year period, they will probably give only $200,000 or $300,000. At the end of that three-year period, because of inflation, that million-dollar building is now going to cost you 1.3 or 1.5 million dollars, and you haven't gotten anywhere. You have wasted money, you have wasted time, you have wasted opportunity, and you may have a failure on your hands rather than a success. So waiting can be counterproductive.

When the people pledge the money, say "hallelujah," thank God, go to the bank, get an interim construction loan, and build. If your church has a sound program and a good financial history, most banks will lend you money based on your pledges. Normally, pledges are not legally binding documents, with each person committed to the bank for a specific portion of the loan; rather, the loan is made to the church corporately. The bank will not technically lend money on those pledge cards, but they will have considerable impact on the bank's decision to lend the church the money.

Once your church has pledged the money or most of the money for the project, should you take out a construction loan and begin building? Absolutely. Show your confidence in the people. They have said they will do it. Believe in them, believe in God, and go for it!

How do you determine the amount of money you can anticipate your people to pledge when all the factors—clear understanding, confidence in leadership, faith in the program, and full information—are just right? Remember that the degree to which those important intangible factors vary will affect that answer.

Assuming all systems are go, here is the way to determine what the people will likely pledge. This is not only in a context of optimum supporting factors, but a general guideline that you may massage up or down because of other factors. We will talk about how many people you can realistically anticipate pledging, but those pledge cards, in an average blue-collar church where everything else is pretty good, will run about $3,000 per pledge card for the entire three years, or $1,000 a year. If the supporting factors are optimal and the church is above average in its socioeconomic status, with professionals comprising one-half to two-thirds of the membership and with maybe three or four really financially successful people thrown in, the pledges can average $6,000 to $8,000 over the three years per card.

I have been a part of only two campaigns that averaged $10,000 to $12,000. In those cases, the above factors were present in a maximum way, plus virtually every person in the congregation was a professional—a doctor, an attorney, an investor, an entrepreneur, a business owner, or a middle to upper management executive.

Generally speaking, Baptists, Bible church members, CMAs, Pentecostals, Charismatics, Wesleyans and Nazarenes tend to represent a cross section of the community, with emphasis toward the middle. Methodists, Presbyterians, and Episcopalians are sometimes a bit more upscale, more upwardly mobile and affluent, and the pledge potential there can be higher, but only if the other supporting factors are high as well. These are only general guidelines, and you can ultimately determine how they relate to your church within the sovereignty of God. With a variation of 10 to 20 percent either way, though, I have found them to be rather consistent predictors of pledging. I have recently consulted with a Baptist church and a Nazarene church throughout their programs. The Baptists were aiming at a $2.7 million program and pledged $2.9 million. The Nazarene church was aiming at $650,000, and pledged $820,000.

Early on, professional fund-raisers used an entirely different method to determine likely giving potential as follows: Select a group of fifteen to twenty persons most likely to be knowledgeable about as wide a cross section of your church membership as possible. Give each of them an individual list of your adult church membership. Ask them independently of one another to write a figure beside each couple or individual among your adult membership. The number they will write is their opinion in response to this question: "If properly motivated to pledge to the campaign, how much could this individual or couple pledge?" Notice that the question is not how much *will* they pledge; it is how much *could* they pledge. Some will know that a person they are evaluating will give absolutely nothing. That is not the question. Remember, it is not a question of how much you think they *will* give but, in your opinion, how much, effectively motivated, they *could* give.

When all the volunteers have marked all the members on their individual lists, the next step is to total each list and find the average dollar figure from all the estimated amounts. Divide that average by a fourth. The total amount pledged will likely be approximately one-fourth of what the group has estimated that the people are capable of pledging. This method was fairly reliable in earlier campaigns, though I have not seen it used in recent years. Some insight might be gained by comparing the result of this method to the result of my method. At least, it would be interesting to see how close the two totals are, and it could provide further support for the proposed campaign.

Let us talk through an average case study. You can then filter this through the unique ministry and situation of your own church and have a reasonable assumption of what might happen. "City Church" is pretty high in the area of the intangibles. They feel good about their church, they understand the program, they love the Lord, they are secure enough to want to reach others, they're prepared to stretch, and they are ready to build. There is no disharmony or perceptible resistance to the building program or to the campaign plan to raise the money.

The campaign is an organized, easily understood three-to-four month effort which involves the people, informs the people, and inspires the people to pledge for its success, and which moves along toward an event, specifically a pledge banquet, at which the goal is to attempt to have the entire Sunday morning adult worship attendance present. The people know they are going to be asked to pledge at the banquet, they feel God's inspiration to do so, they are not surprised, they understand the program, they know why they're there, and they've come to make their commitment.

City Church has a thousand in attendance on Sunday, of whom are approximately seven hundred adults, plus children and teenagers at the banquet. This number, however, can go to eight hundred or more adults who, although not perfect attendees, are present approximately twice a month and are to be counted as regular attendees. The children are not normally part of the campaign, though a special children's party will be provided for them the night of the banquet, freeing their parents to enjoy the evening. Teenagers may or may not be a part of the banquet. They may have their own fellowship, they may serve at the banquet, or they may be a part of the banquet itself. If they do attend, and you choose to give them opportunity to pledge as well, you could estimate the number of teenagers at perhaps fifty to one hundred, and estimate that they might pledge $50 to $100 each for the three-year total. This could be a beautiful, maturing experience for the young people but will not be a significant amount of the overall amount pledged.

This brings us to about eight hundred adults to target, cultivate, inform, and inspire, so that they are present at the banquet. In a well-run campaign, you should anticipate all eight hundred being there. Approximately one hundred could be single adults. Many single adults have excellent jobs, are highly motivated, and will pledge significantly. Generally, however, they tend to pledge less than married couples, except for some older ladies, perhaps widows in the church, who may be financially secure. This is an area that is hard to determine, but I would put a figure of about one-half as an estimate of their pledge in relationship to what the couples will pledge.

The 700 remaining married adults equate to 350 couples. These couples, in an all blue-collar church, will probably pledge about $3,000 each, bringing you to about a million dollars from your couples. However, in virtually every congregation there could be 20 to 30 percent professionals and businesspersons who could be expected to pledge $6,000 to $8,000 per couple.

An unknown group is one I call "the sleepers." There are rather regularly one to five families or individuals that could potentially give a lot of money—$50,000, $100,000, $250,000 or more. I strongly urge you, as pastor and building committee chairman, to visit, work with, and cultivate these members personally in their own homes, lovingly and gently bringing them along, as you prayerfully ask God to touch their hearts to make a significant pledge. Attention to the sleepers can cause your pledge total to rise.

There are also always other precious people in the church whom we tend to underestimate. The quietest, most unassuming family in our congregation is extremely generous every year in our annual mission offering. There are always special factors that might stir the heart of that sweet, older lady in your church who is so quiet and yet so faithful. Perhaps her husband was instrumental in starting the church, perhaps her son who had intended to enter the ministry died in military service, or perhaps she was ministered to in some special way at a sensitive time in her life. Perhaps some quiet older person in your church has a history of quietly giving to colleges and Christian organizations. Perhaps there are some memorializing opportunities. A gymnasium, an office suite, or a chapel named in their honor or in honor of someone they revere might stimulate them to high-level giving. These are just some of the possible factors on the "plus" side of the equation.

I am thinking of a church with which I recently consulted that runs about 1,400 in attendance. All the factors were there, with all of the above ingredients in the mix. It was an ideal situation. In this case, perhaps 60 to 65 percent were businesspersons and professionals, which brought the numbers on up to $6,000 and $8,000 with several $10,000 and $15,000 pledges, and a few in the $100,000 range. The bottom line is this: The membership responded in a very positive way to a successful campaign spearheaded by a greatly loved pastor, and the pledges exceeded the $3.4 million goal for new buildings and new land by nearly $400,000. And, I'm happy to say, this church is currently in the middle of its building program, with the monies coming in ahead of schedule.

Let me be quick to say that you will find some surprises along the way. Some will thrill you, and some will break your heart. I am thinking of a man who pledged $500,000 to something less important than his church and its building program. After much cultivation and encouragement, he pledged only $3,000 to the campaign. But I'm also thinking of a young couple that I felt should not have pledged over $2,000 or $3,000 but who pledged $36,000 and met their pledge. Generally speaking, those two extremes, which may surprise you, will offset each other. Most of the time, there are more positive stories than negative when the Spirit of God is moving in a campaign. But be prepared for one or two people who could give a lot of money, but who give nothing or very little. So factor in maybe $100,000 to $200,000 for the top three or four potential givers who could each give that much, but be prepared, as you cultivate them and pray for them, for the possibility of them doing much less.

Even if all the factors are evident but the entire church is comprised of laborers, $3,000 total pledged over three years should be an average couple minimum, with each single coming in at $1,500 to $2,000. You can, at the same time, allow for the possibility of a handful of $20,000 to $100,000 pledges. You can also know beforehand that the greater the percentage of financially well-to-do people, the more the $3,000 pledges may change to $5,000, $7,000, or even $10,000.

6

BORROWING AND PLEDGING

THE AVERAGE CHURCH IN AMERICA gives $7 per person per Sunday, including those from the nursery to the oldest senior adult. The average Southern Baptist church gives $14. The average so-called megachurch, $27 to $30. Our "across the board congregation" led our denomination in per capita giving with $40 to $45 per Sunday for many years. Today, with the rise of other megachurches reaching primarily the upwardly mobile, such as Second Baptist of Houston, Prestonwood of Dallas, and others, some churches are giving even more than that.

But don't compare your church to the average. What is important is what your people can give. It is very difficult to state a rule of thumb, and those who do so often tend to suggest a higher possibility than may be realistic and raise false hopes for a campaign. Let's try to keep a proper balance of realism and faith at this point.

All things considered, throwing out all the exceptions on the highs and the lows, in an average campaign, a pretty good model is that your people should pledge the equivalent of one year's church budget over and above the existing budget, with the amount to be divided over the three years for the program. In other words, if a church budget is now $1 million a year, over the next three years that membership will contribute $3 million to its operating/missions budget. In a good campaign, pledgers will probably give an additional $1 million spread over those three years, or one-third of a million dollars per year, to the building fund. That means that instead of giving a million dollars each of the three years for the next three years, churchgoers might put a total of $1.33 million per year into the offering plates for the next three years—a million to the church budget and an additional third of a million to the campaign. Professional fund-raisers often promise to raise twice the annual budget. Though they seldom produce it, in some campaigns where all the factors are right and the income of the individual church members is strong, the total can go as high as one and one-half times the annual budget spread over three years. This equates to an additional 50 percent per year.

Now don't get too discouraged or too excited. There are many factors at work, not the least of which are the national economy and employment statistics. At this writing, the economic outlook is strong across the American landscape, but by the time this book comes out, it may be very bad. At one peak time in our economic cycle and church growth history, when all of the influential factors were at their apex, we had an interesting experience that turned into a wonderful blessing.

When we relocated, I promised our people that we would build a family recreation center, but as we continued growing, we found we also needed a new children's building. Each would cost four or five million dollars. What should we do? We agonized over that question for months. Then I felt God speaking gently to my spirit, "Build them both."

I went to the people with a proposal that we would build two buildings by giving two tithes over two years. We called the program "Two-by-Two" and for two years, we asked the people to double up, giving their regular tithe to the budget and an extra 10 percent to the building fund.

Fifteen hundred families in our church signed a pledge card agreeing to do so. The money came in, we built the facilities, and today many of our people continue to give at that rate as the residue of blessings from that experience continues to abound.

What a joy it is to give! But ours is an exceptional story on the high side. Exceptional stories on the low side abound as well. So there's no hard and fast rule. Talk and think these factors through with your leadership and seek the mind of Christ. In answer to prayer, he who holds the future will lead you to a settled, united decision as to what to aim for; it will perfectly match the cost of what he leads you to build at this time, and he will provide the funds. Remember, one successful, pressure-free, positive campaign can lead to another.

If you do good follow-up, you should take in 100 percent of the monies pledged over three years. On the negative side, some people will be unable to pay their pledges. On the positive side, new members will join and compensate, oftentimes providing even more funds than initially pledged during the three year period.

Go to your banker, show him your operating budget, discuss the percentage of that budget currently going to debt retirement, if any, and investigate new ways of structuring your debt, including the possibility of consolidating the new loan to include the current debt.

Whatever arrangements you make, trust the people and trust the Lord. In some cases you should stretch out your loan over five, ten, or fifteen years. In other situations, you should only get a three-year loan and pay it off, leaving the existing indebtedness in place. You don't have to become debt free overnight.

Jesus made no prohibition against borrowing. In fact, he said, "Give to the one who asks you, and don't turn away from the one who wants to borrow from you" (Matt. 5:42). And Paul's admonition in Romans 13:8, "Do not owe anyone anything," has absolutely nothing to do with money. He is talking about paying others the honor and respect we owe them. Additionally, God promised his people in Isaiah that if they were not faithful to him, they would be so financially depressed they would have to ask unbelievers to lend them money. Conversely, he promised if they would honor him, they would be so financially blessed they would have abundance of wealth to lend to others.

Don't let anyone tell you it is a sin to borrow money. That doctrine is a misunderstanding of Scripture. The issue is not debt; it is structuring your debt in such a way as to be prudent and reasonable in its repayment. The red line for a church budget is 30 percent. The amount of money you pay in principal and interest on indebtedness each year should never exceed 30 percent of the amount of money collected for the operating budget of the church, exclusive of special mission offerings. If you are approaching 30 percent already, it may not be time to build. Our own debt percentage is 10 percent, and we are comfortable with that amount.

7

STEPS TO THE SUCCESSFUL CAMPAIGN

THERE ARE FIVE KEYS to a successful campaign, prayer, of course, being the most important. We shall consider the importance and function of prayer separately under the chapters in this book devoted to committees or teams. Choose the team committee or team that best fits your church.

The first key is to *inform the people*. God's people, given the facts, will do the right thing. Arriving at the decision to build, raise the funds, and go forward is one which requires a slow-and-steady involvement of the church's leadership well before the capital campaign begins. The purpose of leadership is to lead. The function of leadership is to get things done. Certainly, God gives the pastor the vision, which he is to cast before the people in the power of the Holy Spirit, but it is important to remember that none of us is infallible. We are indeed prone to error. The writer of Proverbs 1:5 said it well, "A man of understanding will acquire wise counsel" (NASB).

As you seek the Lord for his direction, talk with ministers of education, experienced pastors, and church planners to determine the need for the project and the sequence in which the project should be accomplished in relationship to other needs, such as for other land, buildings, staff, programming, remodeling, or even relocation.

Don't rush. Good plans are the product of good thinking, and good thinking takes time. Involve your senior staff in your planning and deliberations. Consider all the options, and with a good balance of reason and faith, thought and trust, go forward. There are many successful styles of leadership. But again, the purpose of leadership is to lead, and it is a good idea to have a settled confidence in the direction of the Lord for your church before you and the staff begin to involve other church leaders. That is not to say you should ever be dictatorial, stubborn, or overconfident. It is to say that it is wasting the time of your leaders to start completely from ground zero and say, "Does anybody have any ideas about what we should do next?"

As pastor, you should have the ideas, formulated in prayer and consultation, including from the earliest stages the involvement of some of the leadership of your congregation. First, explain the need; second, present the options; and third, lay out a reasonable plan of procedure. Whatever you do, don't force it. Don't push the people. You could be wrong. Be vulnerable at this point. Acknowledge that you have thought this out, discussed it, and prayed over it, but now you are turning to your general leadership to examine it from their perspective. Be transparent and open as they give their input. Be willing to change. Hear all the opinions. Most decisions of this magnitude are formulated with good input, and that certainly includes the best thinking of your own church leaders.

Don't expect or even encourage a decision in the initial meeting. It takes time to think these things through, to build consensus, to pray in community, and to develop a settled confidence that you, as leaders of the church, are prepared to present the plan to the entire congregation. Take your time, jump through the hoops, and go through all the steps.

In our church, the procedure would begin with a dream in the heart of the pastor, discussion with major staff, presentation to the finance and/or building committees, presentation to the deacons, and finally, a call to the church membership for a vote. All of this would normally take three to six months. Try to do it yesterday, and you will fail. Take your time and do it tomorrow, and you will succeed.

All along the way, be completely open. Solicit and seriously consider opinions from every source. Honor those who dissent. They are coming from some place, and that some place may be no place to you, but it is a most important place to them. Those who lived through the Great Depression, for example, may be timid about proceeding. The younger adults who have only known prosperity may likely be more aggressive in their willingness to press forward, but good ideas will often come from those who disagree.

Constantly massage the plan, hear from everybody, confirm the people's agreement at various stages, and reveal all the facts. Adequate information that comes to you from your leadership and goes from you as leaders to the congregation is essential in consensus building, and consensus building brings success. So, the first ingredient beyond prayer is to inform the people. Good information is everything, and the process takes time.

Second, *inspire the people*. Human personhood is comprised of three parts: the mind, the seat of the intellect, where we know; the heart, the seat of the emotions, where we feel; and the soul, the seat of the will, where we commit. Before people choose to follow, to go forward, to commit, and to give, they have to know the right information about the project, be sold on it and believe in it, and they have to feel good about it in their heart of hearts. Preach sermons on winning the lost, building the church, reaching the world. Develop a kingdom mind-set. Get the people to thinking upward and outward. We must be a driven people for the kingdom's sake.

Inspiration comes from three sources: one, the gentle pressure of the Holy Spirit upon the heart to respond to the need; two, the personalizing of the program with testimonies from the people; and, three, persuasive preaching from the pulpit. Tearjerkers are never in order, but persuasive stories from the Bible and real life always are. An inspired people will stretch higher than they can reach. They will dare to trust God for the impossible. They will believe him for big things, and it is that faith which gives substance to dreams.

The third key is to *include the people*. Build a sense of ownership in the congregation. Take time through information and inspiration for the people to feel that it is their dream, not just the pastor's dream. Broaden the opportunity for discussion suggested above from your leadership to your entire congregation. Have a couple of open forums. Solicit questions and comments by inviting members to write, call, fax, and e-mail you. Be among the people—be in their homes, at their dinner parties, and their Sunday school socials. Offer opportunities for the people to approach you with opinions, both dissenting and approving, in informal settings, such as Little League ball games and other casual contact. Walk the halls, stand in the lobby, go to the Sunday school departments. Let everyone feel that the project is *their* project. This assurance comes with information, inspiration, and accessibility or availability. Don't just give the feeling to the people that you care about their opinion. Really care, and they will know it.

Fourth, *involve the people*. In churches with as many as eight hundred to nine hundred in attendance, it may be possible to have virtually every active member on some committee of the capital campaign. The prayer committee, for example, cannot have too many people, nor can the telephone committee. If there are more people than you can place on committees, create new committees. The shut-ins can help you call, the children can help make decorations for the banquet, the teenagers can serve, and everybody can pray. A church that is informed, inspired, included, and involved in the process, and that follows its pastor and believes in the program, is probably in for a great blessing. You may well pledge more than you expected. You can and will be successful.

This is a good place to let your creativity run wild. At one church, each senior adult created a quilt square containing a Scripture and an encouraging word about the success of the campaign. In the event a church's senior adult ministry is too large to make this feasible, you may accomplish the same goal by asking each Sunday school class to create a square. You can display the finished quilt as a backdrop for the banquet and auction it off at a later date, with proceeds going to the building fund.

Another church conducted a Play Dough contest in the children's departments, with each child preparing an entry depicting the future building or related subjects. These are just two ideas. Be creative so that everyone will become conscious of the program, get involved in it, and grow excited about it.

As the enthusiasm builds, don't be surprised when the devil attacks you. Every major program I have ever done in my church was preceded by a few days or weeks of tremendous satanic attack. Just recently, I spoke with a young pastor who is in a state of despondency because everyone in his church was on board for the capital campaign except one influential man who was not even planning to attend the pledge banquet, let alone give anything. Ninety-nine and one-half percent of his people were excited and signed up to attend the banquet, but in his mind everybody was against it. Mark these words, *"The devil can make one sound like a thousand."* Moses had his dissenters, as has every leader in history. No one had greater reason to be discouraged than our Lord. At the critical hour of his life, one doubted him, one denied him, and one even betrayed him. Apparently, John was the only disciple who followed him all the way to the cross. Faint not. Where God leads, God provides. Jesus said when we follow him, we will have trouble. When opposition and problems come, rejoice. It is God's guarantee that you are following the will and way of the Nazarene.

8

PRINCIPLES OF MOTIVATION

I AM OFTEN ASKED, "How do you get people to give?" The answer to that question is similar to the ones for many other questions. How do you get people to pray? How do you get people to come to Sunday school? How do you get them to do anything?

Principle one is *information*. Read the preceding chapter again. Take your time. Hide nothing, reveal everything, honor your critics, answer their questions honestly, and remember that God's people, given the facts, will indeed do the right thing.

Principle two is *enthusiasm*. The word *enthuse* is from the two Greek words *en theos*, meaning simply "in God." The word picture is that of the lesser containing the greater. Like two wildcats in a gunnysack, a person filled with God is excited. Perhaps no more godly characteristic in life exists than enthusiasm. Get excited about giving. Your spirit will be contagious. If you believe in it, they will believe in it. Challenge the people to do the impossible, and remember, if you don't stretch higher than you can reach, it isn't faith. Enthusiasm is an essential ingredient in motivating people to do anything.

Principle three is *illustration*. When you want people to do something, do it yourself. Point out those who are doing it, and let them tell their story. Rick Warren is one of the most successful pastors of our time. In his southern California church, Rick has followed a practice every Sunday for over twenty years. In virtually every sermon, he uses an illustration from the life and experience of someone in his congregation. But Pastor Warren does an amazing thing. Rather than tell the story, he lets the person tell it himself. At the point in the sermon at which he is ready for the testimony, the individual simply rises from the front row or from a chair on the platform, walks to the pulpit, and gives a two-or three-minute prepared testimony.

31

Occasionally the testimony will be on a screen, videotaped earlier, or it will be a videotape of someone in another city. The power of the personal testimony is perhaps the best of illustrations. A testimony that is live, fresh, and happening right now, though it be simple, is more effective than a grand testimony that happened to someone else a hundred years ago.

In the earliest years of my ministry, I listened every Sunday afternoon to Charles G. Fuller on his live nationwide radio broadcast from Long Beach auditorium in California. How scintillating were those *Old-Fashioned Revival Hour* broadcasts! There was the mighty piano artistry of Rudy Atwood, the letters read from Rev. Fuller's dear wife, Honey, and the heart-warming preaching of Dr. Fuller. But the highlight of the program was always the invitation. Apparently, the program attracted many sailors from the nearby Long Beach Naval Base. How many hundreds of times have I been moved to tears, as he said, "God bless you, sailor lad. I see that hand. Yes, sailor boy, I see you coming. God bless you as you come." Not only did I want to come forward and make a decision for Christ, but I'm sure every sailor in the world did as well.

Tell the story, allow the testimony, and point out others who are doing it. Illustration is a powerful part of motivation.

The fourth ingredient in motivation is *repetition*. The primary theme of the preaching of Jesus was salvation. His second most prominent message was stewardship. Think of it. Thirty-one of his thirty-four parables were about money. The master teacher, the consummate motivator, knew the importance of repetition. In testimony and song, in brochure and sermon, in devotional, poster, mail-out, and banner, keep the campaign before the people.

Years ago I walked into a drugstore in Ohio to buy Gillette razor blades. Hanging from the ceiling were hundreds of triangular-shaped fliers advertising peach sundaes. Everywhere I looked, it said, "Peach sundae, 19 cents. Peach sundae, 19 cents." I went back to the razor blade counter, took out two dollars for some Gillettes, and the clerk asked, "What do you want?" I said, "Give me a peach sundae." I didn't want a peach sundae; I wanted razor blades, but they had convinced me I wanted a sundae. Repetition had won the day.

Information, enthusiasm, illustration, and repetition are four God-given tools for the motivator who would be "wise as a serpent and harmless as a dove." Beneath all, around all, above all, and most of all, are the presence and the power of the Holy Spirit that make it happen. So let the breath of God be upon these four principles. Motivation will rise from the hearts of your people, and a successful program will be the result.

9

POINT OF THE PROGRAM

THE PURPOSE OF A FOOTBALL GAME is to win, but the *method* is to get the ball over the goal line. In a capital campaign, the purpose is to pledge needed funds, and the method is to get the people over the goal line of attendance at the pledge banquet. *The entire campaign is about a pledge banquet.* As I write these words, I am just forty-eight hours away from preaching at a pledge banquet for a wonderful Nazarene church with which I have been consulting. By the time the leaders made their decision on what to do and came to me to help analyze the probability of their ability to do it, there were only two months remaining until the beginning of summer, and summer is not a good time for a pledge banquet. "Two months," they asked, "Can we do it?" I helped them examine all the important factors of a successful campaign, determined the ingredients were there at a very high level, and said, "Let's go for it."

The people are really pumped. They have prayed, they have organized, and they have banquet reservations numbering the equivalent of the entire Sunday morning adult worship attendance. The problem with this fine church is not hitting the goal; it's running right past it. To God be the glory.

My point is simple. It can be done in as little as two months. Though many professional fund-raisers recommend six months, I have found that length of time to drag on and on, carrying the possibility of being counterproductive. A church can accomplish its goal in two to three months, but I think three to four is just about right. Anything under that may be pressing it a bit, and anything longer than that may tend to be "draggy" and discouraging.

A test of true intelligence and understanding is one's ability to comprehend the whole. I have been in committee meetings in which we were discussing whether or not to build a $2 million Sunday school building, and someone on the committee asked which way the door would swing in the nursery, or what color would be used to paint the rest rooms. This person completely failed to comprehend the big picture.

So, fine tune your own intelligence and understand me clearly. *The whole campaign is about getting the people to the pledge banquet,* arriving together in a beautiful, positive environment in which the people have been cultivated, informed, involved, and inspired to clearly understand not only the whole program but the specific purpose of the banquet. The evening has but one single purpose—to get every adult church member to the banquet and to get each one to sign a three-year pledge card.

Keep the goal in focus: The start of the game begins with committees (or teams), involvement, information and inspiration. It progresses over a period of three to four months to the winning touchdown, which is a glorious, well-prepared, happy, beautiful, Holy Spirit-anointed pledge banquet at which the people are inspired, hear from God, and willingly and sacrificially respond to his prompting and his program.

Later on, I will have some good suggestions for you about those who do not attend, or who do attend but do not pledge. We will also examine common mistakes and things to avoid in various programs, but, believe me, no greater mistake is made than to build up to the banquet, get everybody excited and not ask them to fill out the card on the spot. If you love the girl , you've courted her, she's expecting you to propose , you want her to say yes, and you know she's ready to say yes, then *pop the question!* If you have executed the campaign well, have delivered a good inspirational message by yourself or a guest speaker, and have gone meticulously through the pledging process in the power of the Holy Spirit as described in chapter 19, *the banquet is the time to ask for the commitment.* Don't even suggest the possibility of people taking the card home, praying about it more, thinking about it, and bringing it back. There are a few who will do that without any encouragement from you. But don't even hint at that possibility until you have finished the evening.

Comprehend the whole; keep the goal line in your mind. There is one plan with many parts, but the purpose is to get the people to the banquet, happy, inspired, informed, and ready to commit. It's all about the banquet! It is the touchdown, and your committees carry the ball toward the victory.

10

ORGANIZING THE CAMPAIGN

YOU ARE NOW READY to appoint your committees or teams. The procedure is as follows: The pastor should prayerfully and thoughtfully name the general chairperson for the steering committee. Ideally, he or she should be the most respected, influential, and godly member of the church. This individual should completely support the program, including the campaign to finance it, and should be gifted in administration, general intelligence, and follow-through. In the event the individual asked to serve is reticent to do so because of lack of administrative and organizational skills, assure your nominee that your help and the help of others so gifted will be available and that the church secretary will assist in the determination, scheduling, and notification of meetings, both steering and individual committees.

The chairperson should, in concert with the pastor and two or three other knowledgeable and insightful people, determine individual committee chairpersons. It would then be wise to sit down with each chairperson to assist in selecting each committee's potential members. Each committee should number five to ten persons, though seven is normally a good number for an effectively functioning committee. You can designate committees to serve as telephone callers, car parkers, and prayer warriors, and they can take on endless other ministries as the needs arise.

Once the pastor and general chairperson, in consultation with two or three other knowledgeable persons, have selected individuals to chair the committees, the general chairperson and pastor should jointly call each potential committee chairperson to enlist that person's service.

Be prepared. While most will accept, some may decline, and it would be wise to make a backup call to another choice, even in the same evening.

Also, be prepared for the fact that some will want a few days to think and pray about it. This, of course, is admirable, but you need to graciously say to them that you're under a bit of a time constraint and need a return call in no more than two or three days with their answer.

When you have selected your chairpersons, ask them to prepare fifteen or twenty names for possible members of their committee. Oftentimes, many of them will select the same names, so urge them to prayerfully consider good people who may not be as immediately recognizable, but are good, solid people who would do a faithful work. Again, the ideal number is probably seven per committee, and all the committees need to be enlisted and on board by the end of the second week from the inception of the campaign.

The chairpersons of each committee will comprise the steering committee. The general chairperson of the campaign is the only member of the steering committee who is not chairing another committee.

The next step is something unique to this program, but something that I think is most helpful. Immediately schedule a meeting of all the committees, and spend an hour or so educating each committee publicly in the presence of all the rest of them about their committee's responsibilities and how they will perform them. The purpose of this meeting is to give every committee member a feel for the entire campaign as a whole, so each has a better sense of how each committee's part fits into the finished product. I prefer to have this meeting not only with the steering committee, comprised of the committee chairpersons, but with the entire individual membership of the various committees as well. This would be a gathering of, more likely, fifty to seventy-five than of eight to ten. We are responding to the need for adequate information and consensus-building. It is essential that the pastor read this book several times before this training meeting in order to have a thorough grasp of the information he or she is imparting.

Each individual on each committee has a sphere of influence. These concentric circles comprise the whole, and as they spread the information about what they are doing and enlist the support of others, they will be able to do so in a context of knowledge of the entire program. This not only builds consensus and confidence, but it allows the individual members to be able to respond to questions and concerns from other church members on the basis of full information. It is incomplete or incorrect information that usually causes the most trouble. Remember, God's people, given the facts, will normally do the right thing, but they do need to have the facts.

11

THE PRAYER COMMITTEE

WE BEGIN WITH THIS COMMITTEE because it is the most important. I do not say that simply because I think it's what you want to hear. I say it because I have experienced prayer's power again and again. In the organization, structure, and execution of the campaign, you are symbolically building an altar. Though it is not made of stones, as was Elijah's on Mount Carmel, it, like his, invites the presence of God in the program. It will take three to four months to get it in place. But the failure or success of the climactic pledge banquet event toward which you will have moved will not depend on the organization the people see but on that which cannot be seen—the power and actuality of the Spirit of God in answer to prayer.

The privilege of leadership carries with it the burden of success. No, it doesn't all rest on the shoulders of the pastor, but most of it does. No, the campaign will not be a success *because* he has devoted himself to four months of prayer, but it will not be a success *unless* he has. Nearly forty years ago, I wrote *The Power of Positive Praying,* destined by the Spirit of God to be a best-seller. Though the book has sold two million copies in six languages over the world, still I learn something new about prayer almost every day.

One of the things I've been discovering lately is this: God blesses everything in your world because you are praying. It is not necessarily true that he gives you the answers to the things for which you are specifically praying, but it is true that because you are praying, he blesses other areas of your life as well. A man or woman of prayer is a blessed person. Somehow, I don't think the Spirit of God will set the people praying unless the pastor is steadily and seriously praying for the movement of God in the campaign.

Somehow, they will know. No matter how many people pray and how much organization happens, God will not be pleased to anoint your campaign with supernatural blessing unless the pastor leads the way in prayer.

Scripture says we will not be heard for our much speaking. Unfortunately, this has far too often become an excuse not to pray very much. The apostle Paul was not discouraging prayer. He was referencing the pagan who substituted endless babble for serious petition to the heart of God. Mark these words: There is a distinct, inseparable link between prayer and the end result of the campaign, and there is an equally inseparable link between quality prayer and the amount of time we spend in prayer. The pastor who would devote time to serious prayer will be a blessed person when the campaign is completed. "But thou, when thou prayest, enter into thy closet, and when thou hast shut thy door, pray to thy Father which is in secret; and thy Father which seeth in secret shall reward thee openly" (Matt. 6:6 KJV).

The prayer committee is a wonderful place to involve your people. It can be as large as you like. The purpose of the prayer committee is, of course, to lift the entire campaign up to God with daily intercession for his power and mighty blessing as he stirs the people to hunger for his heart and will, to hear his voice, and sacrifice for his kingdom.

It is also an important time to pray the protection of God over the pastor and the church against satanic opposition. Satan hates the church, and he especially hates those times when the church is faithfully and courageously stepping out to advance God's kingdom. There will be times of difficulty, distraction, and discouragement, but they are all fiery darts of the wicked one.

Ephesians 6:16–17 reminds us that Satan's attack is deflected through the shield of faith and the sword of the Spirit, which is the Word of God. What does it mean for the prayer committee to lead the people to pray the shield of faith over the church at this important time? It is to agree together in believing faith that God will allow nothing to deter, distract, or defeat His people during this important time of conquest. Remember, we cannot bind Satan, and it is foolish to attempt to do so, but we can and must ask God to bind him. That is his business and his alone, and he will do it if we ask him from hearts of faith.

The other defense against Satan's attack at this vulnerable time is the sword of the Spirit, which is the Word of God. The Spirit will fight the battle for us, but we must place a sword in his hand, and that sword is God's Word. So, we claim the Word, memorize the Word, quote the Word, and pronounce it daily over every facet of the program. This, with the shield of faith, assures Satan's defeat and God's victory as the church builds for tomorrow.

You should plan and conduct three important prayer meetings. They can be in several homes, in one large home, or in the church itself. And remember that the purpose of a prayer meeting is not to sing about prayer, talk about prayer, or have Bible studies on the subject of prayer. The purpose of a prayer meeting is to pray.

Your first meeting should be at the beginning of the campaign. When the committees are enlisted and trained and the people are informed, it's time to pray.

The second big prayer meeting should occur at the beginning of the visitation week, the week the people go into homes to take brochures, explain and answer questions about the program, and ask the people to make reservations for the banquet. (It is essential not to solicit funds in peoples' homes at this time.)

You should conduct the third major prayer meeting around the altar of the church on the Saturday morning preceding the pledge banquet. The ideal time for the banquet is the following Sunday night, and the best time to encourage large numbers of people to pray is on Saturday morning. Many sincere hearts will gather at the altar, sacrificing the pleasures of a leisurely Saturday, to pray fervently the power of God upon the banquet.

Special prayer for the campaign and its success should go out to God in each public service between the beginning of the campaign and the banquet itself. Enlist children to pray. Enlist young people, elderly and single, rich and poor.

Let the committee enlist one person for each service who will simply come to the platform and spend half a minute to a minute praying before the congregation. A prayer chain or prayer clock, which people sign, to ensure that someone is praying around the clock for seven days preceding the banquet, is an important part of the prayer strategy for the church as well.

During the month before the banquet, testimonies in adult Sunday school departments, Bible study groups, or worship services are most effective. These testimonies should not be about how much one is going to give but about how much they believe in the program, how glad they are to be a part, and how they are seeking the heart of God in prayer for his will regarding their pledges. The prayer committee should plan these testimonies. It should prepare the class teacher or departmental director to introduce the individual and follow his or her testimony with a prayer asking God's direction for each member of the class about decisions regarding their individual pledges.

Within virtually every church, certain prayer groups will already exist. The steering committee should determine the leaders of these groups and contact them with a personal appeal to have consistent prayer for the campaign, always reminding the prayer groups as well as the entire congregation that the focus is not primarily about money and campaigns but about Christ and the world for which he died.

Prayer chains, prayer clocks, and countless other plans are key tools to set the people praying. Prayer guides can also be inexpensively printed and distributed to the entire congregation at the beginning of the campaign.

12

THE PUBLICITY COMMITTEE

THE FIRST RESPONSIBILITY of the publicity committee will be to determine the theme for the campaign. Some of the earliest programs used "Together We Build." Hundreds of ideas are possible. The last two with which I have been involved called their campaigns "Faith in Action" and "Journey to Tomorrow." Brainstorm, solicit ideas, think and pray, and get some of your sharp, creative young adults involved. Include singles and teenagers. Pass out forms and have a contest, but early on select a name that's just right for you.

The biggest job, and perhaps most important for this committee, will be designing the brochure. Whatever else you do, don't scrimp either on the brochure or the banquet. The brochure must be professionally designed and printed. This is the centerpiece of the public relations portion of the campaign that your leadership will take personally to the families in your church prior to the banquet. It should inform and inspire, and the quality or lack of it can have a great impact on the success of your campaign.

Again, don't scrimp. The brochure should be creatively laid out, with the help of a professional. It should be 8 1/2 x 11 inches when folded, with three pages printed on each side. It should be high-quality, uncoated stock, 80 to 100 text weight minimum. It should be in full color with great eye appeal. One of the nicest I have ever seen was done by the First Church of the Nazarene in Houston. Pastor Keith Newman and his congregation did a fantastic job in every area of their campaign, particularly this one, and went over and above their goal. (There is a copy of this brochure in this book, on pp. 125–30.)

As in all advertising, white space sells. Don't tell people more than they want to know. A cluttered brochure will not be read, so keep it spread out and appealing to the eye. Again, a professional must help you. The brochure should include no more on the cover than the theme, the name of the church, and perhaps a verse of Scripture. While not attempting to answer everything, the text should answer some basic questions, such as what you are building and why, what it will be used for, how much it will cost, how much you need to pledge, and what the duration of the pledges will be. The brochure should also include a letter from the pastor, sketches of the building, floor plans, a few pictures, and perhaps two or three testimonials of support. Also include a chart showing how much an individual or family may contribute over three years at various levels of weekly, monthly, and annual giving.

The brochures must be designed, printed, and on hand, ready for distribution one month before the banquet. Your invitation committee will personally take them to each home. They are the centerpiece of the program next to prayer and the banquet itself.

While the design and preparation of the brochure is the most important job this committee will accomplish, much other work remains for them as the campaign moves forward. The publicity committee will pursue every means at its disposal to keep the program before the congregation. A banner, tastefully done, with the campaign theme, should be on display in a prominent position somewhere in the church, perhaps above the choir loft.

In addition, the weekly church paper should contain positive testimonies and inspiring information about the campaign and its progress. The paper is also an important tool to disseminate clearly information about schedules and dates.

The four weeks immediately before the banquet will be intense with phone calls and visits, so it is important that the people understand clearly what is happening and when. Remember that one of the principles of motivation is repetition. Gently and consistently keep the plan, the program, and the schedule before the congregation. Here again, creativity is essential. Tabletop prayer reminders, bookmarks, bumper stickers, refrigerator magnets, balloons for the children, key chains—all are of value if they keep the program before the congregation.

The weekly church paper may be your best tool to do this. Additionally, posters, designed in the image of the brochure front with pertinent information regarding the time and place of the banquet, should hang prominently in appropriate places around the building. Bulletin covers for the last four to six weeks should match the brochure cover. The weekly Sunday morning bulletin can also carry a picture and personal testimony of someone who is excited about the campaign. This person, or another, may also give a testimony during the morning services as coordinated with the pastor. (I strongly discourage public testimonies about specific amounts of money to be pledged, but more about that later.)

Being careful to keep consistency of theme, design, and colors in all publicity materials, the committee may choose to print additional tools such as prayer reminders, as coordinated with the prayer committee, to be placed on the kitchen tables of members for mealtime prayers. Preparing and printing of forms, including nursery reservations, banquet reservations, transportation reservations, youth or children's party reservations, prayer request records, preschool emergency contact records, child-care coupons, guided telephone conversations, bulletin inserts, and tabletop prayer reminders, are

---

Commitment Card

Name_____

Address_____ Zip code_____

　　　Understanding that all I/we possess is a gift from God, and that God delights in blessing the obedience of his children,

I/we rejoice in the opportunity to participate in "The Journey."

$_____ Weekly x 156 weeks; or,
$_____ Monthly x 36 months; or,
$_____ As follows:
_____

To be completed by persons making commitments other than cash:

$_____ Approximate value of gift
　　　　　　　　　 Description of gift

_____

$_____ TOTAL   I/we will give my/our gifts on _____

This is a statement of intent and may be modified as circumstances warrant.

---

responsibilities of this committee, along with delivering them to the appropriate committee.

The front of the commitment card should include space for each person's name, address, zip code, and phone number (see example on previous page).

The back side of the commitment card would present the following chart.

It is advisable to reprint this schedule of giving on the back side of the pledge card as it was previously listed on the brochure. It is also the responsibility of this committee to prepare a packet of material to be handed to the host and hostess for each table the night of the pledge banquet. Each packet should contain six envelopes, each with a pledge card and pen to be distributed to each couple or single at their table at the direction of the speaker following the banquet message. Let the publicity committee take very seriously the importance of its responsibility. To adequately publicize the good news about our church's effort to spread the good news is, along with prayer, the very heart of getting people to the banquet and ready to pledge.

Typical Commitments You Can Make Over a 156-Week Period

Weekly	Monthly	Annually	3-Year Total
2,000	8,660.00	104,000	312,000
1,000	4,330.33	52,000	156,000
500	2,166.67	25,000	78,000
300	1,300.00	15,600	46,800
100	433.33	5,200	15,600
75	325.00	3,900	11,700
60	260.00	3,120	9,360
50	216.67	2,600	7,800
40	173.33	2,080	6,240
30	130.00	1,560	4,680
25	108.33	1,300	3,900
20	86.67	1,040	3,120
15	65.00	780	2,340
10	43.33	520	1,560
8	34.67	416	1,248
5	21.67	260	780

13

THE TELEPHONE COMMITTEE

By four weeks before the pledge banquet, everything should be printed, organized, and ready for distribution. Week four before the big event is "Blast-off Week," and this is when the telephone committee moves into action. Just before this crucial week, the pastor and general chairperson should together write the membership to tell them what will be happening in weeks four, three, two, and one, with an appeal to prayerfully and joyfully receive the callers and visitors, assuring them of no in-home solicitation. Having determined the number of households, married couples, and adult singles, each telephone caller should be assigned five to fifteen calls. The ministry of the telephone callers, often a wonderful project for faithful senior adults, is to prayerfully and cheerfully call the names on their lists during week four before the campaign.

The telephone committee will have prepared four items for each caller: a list of names, phone numbers, report cards, and two suggested scripts printed on both sides of one sheet of paper.

The first script is a sample guided conversation sheet of what to say during their first call in week four. The second delineates what to say during week one, when they call back after the visitors with brochures and invitations to the banquet have been in the home during countdown weeks three and two. I strongly urge that callers do not leave messages on recorders, except a cheery greeting with a word that you will call back. It is important to keep trying until you can have a live conversation with the persons you are calling.

The purposes of the initial call in countdown week four are, first, to tell your people a little about the campaign and to emphasize how much you want everyone to be at the banquet. Second, you can urge them to stay home evenings during the visitation week, since invitation teams will be by their homes. Third, it is important to assure them that there will be no solicitation for funds or any attempt to get signed pledge cards during the home visit. The visit's purpose is simply to inform the people about the campaign, present the brochure, attempt to minister to any spiritual needs the family may have, and sign them up for the banquet.

The second call to the same list of persons is made during countdown week one, immediately before the banquet. Counting down in reverse weeks four, three, two, and one, week four is the initial call saying the visitors are coming. In weeks three and two, in-home visits are made, and in week one, follow-up calls occur just before the banquet. There are two purposes to the follow-up call in week one. The first is to get a telephone commitment for reservations to the banquet from any who did not fill out a reservation form when the visitors came to their homes, or who have not yet mailed one back, or who have not yet made a reservation by any other means. For those who have committed to come to the banquet, the second purpose of the call is a reminder and a word about how excited you are that they are coming to the banquet.

The telephone committee should prepare the lists of five to fifteen names and phone numbers and get from the publicity committee a guided conversation sheet to follow for each of the telephone calls. The committee should put the names, phone numbers, and guided conversation sheets into one packet per caller and give them to each one with a reminder to begin calling on Monday night at the beginning of week four before the banquet, with follow-up calls made during week one.

You will need to schedule two training sessions for the telephone callers. Encourage everyone to attend the first training session, without announcing until it is concluded that there will be a second session for those who were unable to attend the first session.

The following is an excellent guide for the callers:

- Read over the entire script so you can get a comprehensive understanding of the process.
- Conversations one and two are for use during week four, before the visitation times. You are contacting people to see if they received a letter about the banquet from the pastor, to remind them that a member from your church will be coming by their house within the next two weeks

to give them an important packet of information about the upcoming banquet, and to ask that the visitors be graciously received.

- Conversations three and four are to be used during week one, after the visitation weeks, during the follow-up phone calls. You are contacting people a second time to make sure they have received the packet of information and, if not, to verify their address so that you can make sure that they get it. You can also make a final effort to get a banquet reservation.
- You will have three sheets of paper in your packets: (1) a list of names, addresses, and phone numbers, (2) a report form, and (3) a guided conversation sheet. As you reach each family (either a person or an answering machine) write each name on the report form. Verify each address. You need to write down their address only if it is different from your list.
- If you reach a person, proceed through each question and, according to how the person responds, follow the applicable guided conversation.
- If you reach an answering machine, use conversation two or four, depending upon which phone week it is.
- Keep upbeat in your attitude and speak clearly. Your involvement in calling really helps to initiate a sense of excitement.
- Ask for God's strength and patience and make your calling fun! Remember that you are an important part of building God's kingdom.

GUIDED CONVERSATION NUMBER ONE—WEEK FOUR

Caller: Hello, this is (your name) from Houston's First Church of the Nazarene. I am calling on behalf of our pastor and the "Journey to Tomorrow" campaign to remind you that a member from our church will be coming by your home in the next two weeks to bring you an important packet of information about our building program and the banquet on Sunday night, May 3, at 6:00 P.M. Did you get the letter from the pastor inviting you to the banquet?

If the Response Is Yes

Caller: Good. I hope you and your family will be able to attend. There will be a reservation card in the packet brought to your home. We hope you will complete the card and return it to those visiting that very evening so we can make our arrangements for the banquet.

If the Response Is No

Caller: I'm sorry. I will call the office and be sure they send you a copy of the letter so you can understand more about the program and upcoming banquet. Let me be sure we have your correct address. Is it (address)? The team visiting you will bring an important packet with detailed information. There will also be a reservation card, which we would like for you to complete and return that evening to those visitors so we can make our arrangements for the banquet.

Further Information for Both Responses

Caller: There will also be a children's party for boys and girls five years old through fifth grade and child care for infants through preschool at the church that evening, as well as a party for teens (if you choose to have one).

Do you have any questions? (If there is a question, answer if you can or let them know that you will get an answer and call them back.)

We are really excited about what God is doing in our church. We need this new Children and Youth Ministries Center to expand the ministry of Houston's First Church of the Nazarene. Thanks for your time. I will look forward to seeing you at the banquet. If you have any questions, please feel free to ask the person who visits with you in the next couple of weeks or call the church office at (phone number). Good-bye.

GUIDED CONVERSATION NUMBER TWO—WEEK FOUR ANSWERING MACHINE MESSAGE

Caller: This is (your name) from Houston's First Church of the Nazarene's "Journey to Tomorrow" campaign to remind you that a member from our church will be coming by your home in the next week to bring you an important packet of information about the banquet on Sunday night, May 3, at 6:00 P.M. If you have any questions about this visit or the church-wide banquet on May 3, please call me. My phone number is (your number). Thanks. Good-bye.

GUIDED CONVERSATION NUMBER THREE—WEEK ONE FOLLOW-UP CALL

Caller: This is (your name) again from Houston's First Church of the Nazarene. Did someone stop by your house to deliver that packet of information about the "Journey to Tomorrow" banquet?

If the Response Is Yes

Caller: Great! Did you fill out the registration card for the banquet and turn it in?

If this Response Is Yes

Caller: Good! The banquet begins at 6:00 P.M. sharp, so please leave early enough to give yourself plenty of time to fellowship and find your table. Also, the church will open for child care at 5:00 P.M. Do you have any questions? (If there is a question you cannot answer, tell them you will find out and call them back, or they can call the church office.)

Caller: I am looking forward to the banquet and seeing you there. Good-bye.

If the Response Is No

Caller: May I make the reservation for you now? Number of adults attending? Number of children attending? Name and ages? Special transportation needs? Nursery reservations? Thanks for your confirmation. The banquet begins at 6:00 P.M. sharp, so please leave early enough to give yourself plenty of time to fellowship and find your table. Also, the church will open for child care at 5:00 P.M. Do you have any questions? I hope to see you at the banquet. Good-bye.

Or If the Response Is No

Caller: I'm sorry. Let me be sure we have your correct address. Is it (read from your list)? I will send a packet to you immediately.

Caller: One of the important items in the packet is the reservation card for the banquet on May 3 at the Greenspoint Wyndham Hotel with guest speaker Dr. John Bisagno from Houston's First Baptist Church. Also, we are having a children's party for ages four through fifth grade and child care for infants through preschoolers. Both will be staffed by adults, so you won't need to worry about your children's safety or well-being. May I make the reservation for you now? Number of adults attending? Number of children attending? Names and ages? Special transportation needs? Nursery reservations? Thanks for your confirmation. The banquet begins at 6:00 P.M. sharp, so please leave early enough to give yourself plenty of time to fellowship and find your table. Also, the church will open for child care at 5:00 P.M. Do you have any questions? I hope to see you at the banquet. Good-bye.

If the Response Is Still No

Caller: Well, if anything changes, even at the last minute, please be sure to come on.

GUIDED CONVERSATION NUMBER FOUR—FOLLOW-UP CALL ANSWERING MACHINE MESSAGE

Caller: This is (your name) again from Houston's First Church of the Nazarene. I'm sorry I missed you. My phone number is (your number). I am calling on behalf of our pastor and the "Journey to Tomorrow" campaign to make sure someone got by your house to deliver the packet of information about the campaign and to confirm your reservation for the banquet on May 3. Please call me if you have not made your reservation or if you have any further questions. Bye!

In week four, the telephone committee has called the homes to say the visitors are coming. In week three, the visitors have gone to the homes, and in week two, they have made repeat calls to those who were not at home. Week one is the second week for the telephone callers. This, as stated, is the week just prior to the Sunday night banquet.

On Monday night of week one, begin calling the people who either were never contacted at home or who were contacted but indicated they would not be attending, as well as those who simply did not make a promise to attend the banquet when the visitors dropped by. As you attempt to get a last-minute commitment from the undecided or the refusals, leave them with the understanding that if something changes at the last minute, they can still come, even without a reservation. Tell them you'll be praying that the Lord will work it out that somehow they can come, and that you'll be looking for them. Each day of week one, the telephone committee should report to the banquet committee any modifications to the list of people who have made banquet reservations.

As telephone callers, be prayerful, kind, understanding, upbeat, cheerful, and persistent. Yours is a tremendously vital link in the chain of success that will one day result in a beautiful new building for the glory of God.

14

THE INVITATION COMMITTEE

AT NO TIME DO WE WALK CLOSER to our Lord and in his perfect will than when we go into the world in his name. The persons to whom this committee will go in the spirit of the Great Commission are not unbelievers but fellow church members who will help us fulfill the Great Commission through the expansion of the church in the building program. It will be the goal of the invitation committee to attempt to pay an in-home visit to every member of the congregation—singles, married couples, and families. You will need to use discretion in whether to make a visit to the homes of attending children or teenagers whose parents are not members of the church.

As briefly mentioned in chapter 13, the pastor and campaign director will have jointly written the entire congregation, and the publicity committee will have thoroughly publicized the fact that the purpose of the in-home visit is not to solicit money, but to bring the brochure and visit with the family about the program.

This letter should go out in time to be received by the members before Monday of countdown week three, the first of the two in-home visitation weeks. Following is some sample text:

Dear (personalized name):

I am so excited about what the Lord is doing in our church as we move toward our All-Church Pledge Banquet in just a few weeks. In preparation for that, our Invitation Teams will be in the homes of our entire church family next week. Their purpose is to deliver to you our new brochure describing our building program and capital campaign, to make a banquet reservation for you and your family, and to learn how we may pray for you.

Please know that they are not coming to ask for your pledge to our campaign. In fact, no pledge cards will be taken early, and there will be no in-home solicitations! We just want you to have all the details about our church's vision for the future so you may pray more intelligently for our church. So, as our church visitors come to your home this next week, please receive them as you would welcome the Lord into your home. What a wonderful church family we have! I am convinced that together as a church we will grow deeper in love with Jesus and one another.

I am proud to be your pastor and look forward to what the Lord has in store for us together as we "Possess the Land."

In His Bonds,
Your Pastor

The committee should first determine the number of visits to be made. Ideally, enough invitation teams should be enlisted and trained so that no team is responsible for more than five visits. That, of course, is an ideal number, but, in fact, often each team may need to visit seven or eight homes. In no case, though, should any team visit more than ten members' homes.

The first visitation by the teams is week three, as you count down toward the banquet. During week four before the visitation actually begins, counting down toward the banquet, the telephone committee calls everyone to tell them to be expecting a visit from the invitation team next week, in week three. They should ask the members of the church to receive the teams with courtesy and gladness. They should reassure the members that the teams are coming to present them a brochure and to answer questions about the campaign, but that they will not bring a pledge card or ask for a pledge in their homes. It is not possible to overstate the importance of making this clearly understood to those who will be visited.

In week four, the telephone committee makes the calls asking the people to be home next week and to expect an in-home visit by the team. Week three is the week during which the invitation teams go to the homes. The invitation committee should give daily updates to the banquet committee, with names of attendees. Week two is reserved for follow-up visits to absentee members who were unable to be contacted during week three. During week one, the telephone committee will again call confirming the reservations of all of those who committed to come to the banquet during the in-home visitation as well as asking the people who did not commit to reconsider and come on anyway. Hopefully, they can get a reservation commitment over the phone, but if not, they will need to assure the ones they call that they can come with or without a reservation if things change at the last minute.

The invitation teams should consist of a married couple, two men, or two women. One person can make the visit, but there is a great deal of confidence and reassurance generated when two go together, and that is the way our Lord told us to go, is it not?

The question arises as to whether the invitation teams should call the people on their list to request appointments and to tell them they are coming. This can be done either way, but I usually suggest that the visits be made without any prior call to request an appointment, other than the generic call by the telephone committee saying that the teams will be coming, asking the people to be home that week and to receive the teams gladly. The invitation team will, of course, be prayed up, dressed up, smiling, and happy, ready to go and represent their Lord and their church.

In their possession will be a packet of several items that will have been prepared by the publicity committee: the major brochure explaining the building program for which the church is pledging money, a banquet reservation form for individuals to sign indicating the names and number of those attending, a form to record the number and names of the children to be attending the children's party, an emergency contact form to be left with nursery staff on the banquet evening, and a form to list the names and ages of children requiring prekindergarten child care. The invitation team should also explain that in the event a couple says they do not wish to take their child to the nursery, the church will furnish child care coupons covering the expenses of the in-home child care which a young couple may wish to provide themselves.

An additional form will be a special transportation request indicating any needs for personal transportation. This provides a needed service to the elderly, teenagers attending without their parents, those who do not wish to drive at night, the physically challenged, and others. The form should indicate the name, address, and phone number of the individual, the type of transportation required, and the time the driver will arrive for the individual to facilitate arriving at the banquet center fifteen minutes prior to the time it begins. Additionally, the packets will contain a reservation form for teenagers to attend the pizza party, unless the steering committee, the children's committee, and the youth workers have previously decided that they should be at the banquet as wait staff or guests.

A final form will be a personal spiritual concern record. It provides an opportunity for the invitation team to report to the pastor any personal requests for prayer, spiritual needs, or problems which the family may be experiencing. The visitors should not complete it in the home but in the car after the visit is made, and then give it to the pastor.

Remembering that the purpose of the visit is to present a brochure, answer questions, raise confidence levels, and explain the program to the individuals, along with getting their reservations to attend the banquet, the invitation team should be well versed by the steering committee, pastor, and general chairman on all the questions that may be anticipated, both pro and con, from those individuals.

When making a visit, it is always better to ring the doorbell rather than knock on the door. The pleasant sound is reassuring. The opening greeting should be (and you must already know the family's names and those of the children), "Hi, Bill and Mary. We're John and Bob from the church." The next question always concerns how to get inside. The answer is simple. You ask. "Hi, Bill and Mary. We're Bob and John from the church. May we come in?" When you are in, be observant. One person may need to answer the door, turn down the TV, or help take care of the little ones, but, hopefully, both of you can sit on a couch near the family.

Begin with a cheery word about how grateful you are for the joy of visiting them tonight and that you're here to present them with a gift of a brochure about the program, explaining it to them and answering any questions they might have. Walking through the brochure is something the invitation team should rehearse on one another before the call is made. Allow plenty of time to hear questions, give honest answers, and hear criticisms or concerns the family may have. If you do not know the answers, assure them that the pastor or chairman will get back with them and will do their best to try to answer that particular question.

When the family has made their comments or asked any questions, ask them then for a commitment to attend the banquet. Hopefully they will say yes and sign the reservation card for the banquet, which the invitation team will have in their packets. If they should say no, tell them, "Well, we understand, but we do want you to know that in the event things change, you can still decide to come at a later date, and we'll be back in touch with you about that." Don't pressure the family, of course, and leave the door open for the possibility of a reservation at a later date, when either the team or the telephone committee checks back with them.

For those who were not at home during the first week, the invitation team should, of course, return the second week, or even two times during the second week. Saturday mornings are very good times to catch people at home, by the way. Determine whether the family has any child-care needs, tell them about the in-home child-care coupons if they prefer that option, and fill out the appropriate forms such as those for the children's party and any special transportation and spiritual needs they have.

As you finish your visit, tell the family that you want them to know from the bottom of your heart that the church has two great concerns, one being that of reaching new people for Christ, and the other that of graciously ministering to those who are already part of the congregation. Ask them if there are any particular problems, prayer concerns, or needs that the family may have about which you could speak with them and pray for them. After a brief time of discussion, ask if you may lead in prayer and bow your heads and pray. In your prayer, thank God for the joy of having been graciously received by the family and ask God's blessing upon the banquet, and then thank God for the privilege of being a part of the church family and contributing together as brothers and sisters in Christ to the advancement of the kingdom. Leave the brochure and take with you the various reservation slips for the banquet, the children's party, youth party, the nursery, special transportation needs, and prayer requests for personal needs the family may have, remembering to bring the last form out of your packet and fill it out only *after* you have left the home. Turn each of the forms in to the appropriate committee within the next day or two, giving the pastor the information about the personal needs and prayer requests.

A final suggestion, in the event that recruiting invitation teams has proved to be difficult: To lighten the load, committee members can each complete their reservation forms at a joint committee meeting, held on the Sunday evening before week four. This is acceptable, but it is preferable that *every home have a personal visit.*

Your invitation committee, along with every other intricate part of the program, is extremely important, and God will give you a great blessing as you go. You will likely find the following to be true: It will be very difficult to make that first call, but once you have, it will be very difficult to stop. You'll probably be calling the invitation committee at the end of the first week and asking for more names! It will indeed be a joy, and God will bless you richly.

15

THE BANQUET COMMITTEE

THE BANQUET COMMITTEE should be primarily women, with one as chairperson who has a reputation as a gifted entertainer and hostess. Being on this committee is a lot of fun. You're the ones who will put together a beautiful evening, a very special event in which God can work, moving in the hearts of his people and bringing to fruition a wonderful campaign. The first responsibilities of your committee will be to choose the location and set the date. I do not list one before the other in order of importance, because they are inseparably linked together.

The ideal date may not be available for the ideal place, in which case you may have to settle for the best date at the second best site or vice versa. Which should take precedence? Probably the date. The beauty of the surroundings and the convenience of the location are probably secondary to the best time.

Let me emphasize the importance of the *pledge banquet being precisely that,* and not just another church event in the main sanctuary. Yes, it will cost you more, but it is worth more to create a memorable evening in the life of the church, a night the people will never forget, a beautiful and festive evening of joyous commitment to the work of the Lord, leaving a fragrance that will linger in the hearts of the people throughout the three-year duration of the pledges and will contribute to their faithfulness.

I have spoken at many pledge services that were simply a warmed-over Sunday night service, and much was lost. This halfhearted effort is not different it is not special, and if the attendance does not fill the sanctuary, as often happens, the people may sit toward the back with a feeling of disconnectedness that can be fatal. If you have reservations for 180, you can set up tables for 180. If a thousand, then tables for a thousand. When every seat is filled and there is a physical connectedness between the speaker and the people, something special happens. By all means, spend the extra money and have a special dinner.

If you call your dinner a banquet, make it a banquet. Don't have a potluck supper or a catered barbecue, and above all, *don't make the people serve themselves*. Don't use plastic plates and forks. Use tablecloths and silver, with nice china and fresh floral centerpieces.

One of the nice approaches I have found is to have the banquet catered at a nearby hotel. A ballroom, large conference room, or dining hall can serve very well. Give careful attention to the sound system, the seating, the decor, the service, and the menu. Making the banquet special says the program is special, and that helps make the giving special. A potluck supper in the church basement will probably get you potluck results. *Eating* banquets are much more conducive to *giving* banquets. If the young people of your church are willing to be trained to do the serving, perhaps you can save money by not hiring waiters and waitresses, but if your teenagers serve, they should be well-trained and uniformly dressed.

The best night is Sunday. Other nights are acceptable, but only as second-best. Whatever you do, don't have it on Saturday. If you select a Sunday night, the starting time should be 6:00 P.M. Weeknight banquets should start at 7:00 P.M. Six-thirty is not quite the banquet hour, and 7:30 will get the people out too late. Seven o'clock on a weeknight, though acceptable, is a bit less than ideal. Somehow Wednesday nights never seem to have the right feel about them. In most people's minds, Wednesday is not as special as Sunday. I would always choose a Monday, Tuesday, or a Thursday before a Wednesday, with Monday being first choice if you cannot find an acceptable Sunday night. Fridays are not good—there are too many secular activities, school events, and ball games to compete with a banquet. If you choose Monday, be sure to cancel your Sunday evening service.

Choosing the best time of year is also crucial to your success. Summers can be difficult. People are gone. There are many holidays. Vacations abound, and people are generally distracted. A spring campaign should hold its banquet between the middle of April and early to mid-May. Don't plan one beyond that time. There will be too many other distractions, though Sunday does help to avoid this conflict. Considering all the factors, you may conclude late spring is a great time for a banquet.

Another good time for a banquet is the fall. Late October to mid-November can be just right, but no later. Beyond that are Thanksgiving and Christmas, and the people are thinking about other things.

So the ideal banquet would be at 6:00 P.M. on Sunday night, spring or fall. Remember that a May banquet means a January or February beginning. A November banquet means an August or September beginning. Determine which season of the year is most conducive to turning aside from other traditional church programs and focusing on the campaign. Set your date accordingly, ideally on a Sunday night in early May or mid-November.

Where should the banquet be held? I suggest three possibilities: a hotel, a public place such as a lodge or a dining facility at a civic institution, or another church's recreational or dining facility.

I urge you to move from the church in the spirit of specialness. If you hold it at church, your people will have to do much more in cooking, cleaning, and nursery work. The banquet is an event not *by* the people; it is *for* the people. Let all the people—cooks, nursery workers, cleanup crews, and every other member—be in attendance at the banquet. Let them dress up and celebrate, be served and participate.

A hotel is the location of choice. Holding the banquet at a hotel will make it special. If a nice hotel with good food and good service at a reasonable price is not available within a reasonable distance of the church, then consider a civic center or, better still, another larger church that would help you in your campaign by letting you use their facilities. For a predetermined fee, they may even furnish nursery facilities and workers, cooks and servers, and other necessary helpers.

How far away from the church is too far? Think of the answer more in terms of time than distance. Fifteen miles on freeways and highways can seem closer than three or four miles through congested areas. Ideally, the facility should be as near as possible to the building to which the people are accustomed to attending church. The banquet committee should bring a recommendation to the steering committee for final approval.

It is essential to determine costs and sign contracts as early as possible. The time, date, and location of the banquet are some of the primary features to be promoted by the publicity committee, so you should confirm them as soon as possible. It is usually not necessary to provide extra seating and food for those who may come without a reservation. Normally that number is offset by no-shows. But do be prepared to have a few extra chairs set up and extra food served, just in case. And be sure to negotiate the best possible arrangement in this matter and its cost with the hotel management in advance if a hotel and/or catering service are used.

The people should enter a beautiful room. Of course, the decorations will not be gaudy balloons and crepe paper but should be tastefully done with beauty befitting the occasion. Fresh flowers donated a members of the congregation are a nice touch at each table. And, of course, background music should be playing as the people enter, are seated, and the dinner begins. A pianist, organist, group, CD, or tapes are each appropriate. The beauty of using recorded background music, though, is that even the musicians of the church can relax, be served, and enjoy the evening, focusing on pledging their part to the campaign.

Tables should always be round, if possible, with no more than five couples plus the host couple seated at each. Three or four couples plus the host couple is ideal. When the people have been seated, the campaign chairperson should welcome the people and call on someone other than the pastor to lead in prayer. It is important to work with your servers to see that people receive their food quickly and efficiently. The last thing you want is to spoil this night by dragging it out. If the speaker gets up to speak and lead the people in pledging after they are tired and wanting to go home, you have lost the battle. Better too soon than too late. Better they leave wishing for more than less.

Whatever you do, don't ask the people to go to serving lines and serve themselves. That takes away from the specialness of the occasion and belies the concept of a banquet. The people should be served at their tables. Remember, the specialness of the evening translates very readily into the specialness of the *pledging*.

Salads and dessert should be at the tables, not brought to the tables. Serving them takes more time and causes more confusion. Having them already at each table means, of course, that you cannot have frozen desserts such as ice cream that will melt. Time is of the essence. You want to move as quickly as possible through the welcome and invocation, and into the introduction of the speaker. It is not necessary to wait until everyone has finished eating to begin the program. And even if it means paying extra, hire enough waiters to get the tables cleared very quickly. All of this maximizes the fluidity and efficiency of the evening.

The program should feature a master of ceremonies, probably the campaign chairman and not the pastor. All the pastor should do is bring the message or introduce the one who will. It is not necessary to give an overview of the campaign. The attendees have already been through the campaign, and that's old news. Nor is it desirable to introduce every individual campaign committee chairman or member. Simply ask all of them to stand together and give them a round of applause, expressing appreciation for a job well done. Following that, have one brief testimony, introduce one special musical number and the speaker. Another chapter will deal with the message and a detailed outline of how to proceed from that through the filling out and receiving of the pledge cards.

It may be that as a pastor, you are comfortable bringing the message yourself, but, again, you can enhance the specialness of the evening by bringing in someone who is experienced in this area. Don't try to save money here. The time of the men who are gifted at doing this is very valuable, and they should be financially compensated as such. Cut corners in your choice of speaker, and much is lost.

Pastor, please note that your last great opportunity to reach your congregation is on the Sunday morning of the pledge banquet. Let the ushers have banquet reservation cards in hand (don't insert them in the bulletin). At a key spot in the morning service, positively underscore how excited you are about the program, how great the banquet will be, how many are coming thus far and how much you want them to be there. Then say, "How many of you have not been able to make a reservation before now? Please raise your hand. We want you to be a part of the entire church family so much." Have the ushers give them a banquet reservation card at that point. Do this far enough in advance of the offering that you can ask the people to fill them out and place them in the offering plates as they come by their row.

The banquet committee should go to an office and take out the reservation cards immediately and make arrangements to add that extra number. Don't be discouraged if you didn't have the number of commitments by Saturday that you would have liked to have had. This Sunday morning number could possibly add as much as 5 to 6 percent to the total number.

Thursday night before the banquet, the banquet committee chairpersons should meet with all hosts and hostesses and give each a master list of attendees. Hosts and hostesses should choose an appropriate number of guests to sit at their table, being careful to select some with whom they are not acquainted. Friday and Saturday, hosts and hostesses should call everyone at their table with an encouraging word about how excitedly they are looking forward to welcoming them. By Sunday morning, the host and hostess committee will prepare charts for the lobby of the banquet hall listing table numbers, hosts and hostesses, and guests. The transportation/

parkers/greeters committee should get copies of these charts on Sunday morning, so that they can familiarize themselves with the hall layout before guests arrive. The greeters should place them in the lobby of the banquet hall so they can direct banquet attendees to their assigned table.

16

THE CHILDREN'S COMMITTEE

IT WILL BE THE RESPONSIBILITY of this committee to do three things. The first is to make arrangements for the smaller children. Nursery or preschool care for children under age four is of utmost importance. Very few people will voluntarily provide care at home for their little ones in order to attend a pledge banquet. In the event, however, some choose to do so, offer coupons to those young couples who wish to use them, for which the church will simply reimburse them for their in-home baby-sitters.

The arrangements for those for whom the church will provide child care can allow for much flexibility. If the church to which the parents normally take their little ones is near the banquet facility or if you actually use your own facility for the banquet, then, of course, use your own nurseries. It is important, however, that this committee begin enlisting outside workers to staff the nurseries on that evening. You want your nursery workers to be at the banquet, not in the nursery. Typically, this will mean employing nursery workers from other churches that do not have Sunday night services and will normally require that you pay them a higher hourly rate than they receive for Sunday morning hours because many of them will not easily be hired away from their Sunday night family time to come and work for you.

Another possibility is that you could employ the nursery workers at a similarly increased hourly wage at a nearby church, or at the church you are using if you hold your banquet at another church, or near a hotel or civic center. But do what you must to provide quality preschool child care for your young couples at no cost to them, while still offering the highest possible levels of safety, convenience, and confidence in the hearts of the young parents.

The second responsibility of the committee is to arrange a children's party for the first- through sixth-graders. Actually, these may be two parties in the same building, given the varying interests of fourth- through sixth-graders from those of first- through third-graders. Food, recreation, movies, popcorn, and clowns make a fun evening for the elementary school kids of the church. By the way, families who are not church members often ask if they can attend the party and/or the banquet. The answer is decidedly yes.

The third responsibility of the committee is to determine whether to use the youth as ushers, to invite them to the banquet as participants, or to provide a similar party for them. Some churches choose neither to involve the youth in the program nor in a separate party. Make this decision in consultation with the youth leaders and steering committee. Participating can be a good learning opportunity for the teenagers. Pledging five dollars or even a hundred dollars will not only mean something to the campaign but to the young lives who pledge it as well.

17

THE TRANSPORTATION-PARKING-GREETERS COMMITTEE

THESE THREE COMMITTEES may be separate or may be one larger committee overseeing three distinct functions. The purpose of this committee is four-fold: Transport the people, park the cars, greet the people, and seat the people. Remember that several things have been taken by the visitors to the homes during weeks three and two. Inside each packet were the items already described: the brochure, a card for prayer requests, a reservation card for the banquet, a form for reservations for the preschoolers and one for the children's party, as well as a request for special transportation or other needs.

This committee chairman should work with the invitation committee to set up a simple system by which to pass on transportation requests to the transportation-parking-greeters committee. A committee member will call each person who requested special help with transportation to confirm the kind of transportation needed—whether chairlift, ramp, or other require-ment. The committee person will get exact directions to the home and will specify the time at which the driver will be at the door. The goal is to have the passengers arrive fifteen to twenty minutes early.

The parking portion of the committee should meet at the place where the banquet is to be held and study entrances and exits to determine how many parking spots attendees will need, and they will also plan traffic control for entrances and exits. They should meet on Saturday morning with the volun-teers they have recruited to park the cars and practice the procedure. In all likelihood, you will also require a minimum of two policemen to coordinate parking and to get the people on and off public roads.

Parking attendants should be at the parking lot one and one-half hours before the banquet begins, equipped with fluorescent armbands and flashlights. Volunteers should park people as near the entrance to the banquet hall as possible, giving special consideration to the physically challenged, the elderly, and parents who may have brought children.

The greeter's portion of the committee is equally important. These should be people with smiling faces, warm hearts, and outgoing personalities who are excited about the program, love the Lord, and are eager to welcome his people and make them feel comfortable. They will receive seating charts from the host and hostess committee on Sunday morning and will display them before guests arrive. On Sunday evening, greeters should be outside the banquet hall in the lobby and beyond, or even a few steps onto the parking lot, welcoming the people and engaging them in conversation as they enter a beautifully decorated facility in which bright music is playing. Be attentive to any special needs. Offer to carry little ones or babes in arms, push wheelchairs, carry purses, point out rest room facilities, and lead them to their tables, but don't rush them. Tables will have been preassigned with each table host and hostess knowing the names of the four or five couples who will be at their table.

During the evening, let the greeters be observant, functioning as well-trained ushers in a church service. Where there are needs, initiate meeting those needs, watch for problems, and offer to help. If someone has brought a small baby, offer to hold the baby. If the child starts crying during the evening, go to the table and say, "May I take care of him for you?" The responsibility of the greeters is to be warm, hospitable, and helpful, meeting any and every need that may arise during the course of the evening.

At the conclusion of the banquet, as the people exit the facilities, repeat your original greeting procedure. While it is not necessary that the greeters help the same people out, as their seats may have been scattered throughout the hall, it is important that they help *some* people in exiting the facilities. A cheery "good night," a warm smile, or an offer to help escort people to their cars is important.

The entire three-in-one committee, with the exception of employed policemen, will all be inside participating with their families in pledging during the banquet. At the conclusion of the banquet, they should be dismissed early, but only just before the final benediction, in order to help the people to exit the building as comfortably as they entered.

Persons with the gifts of organization and administration will organize, lead, and administer the transportation-parking-greeters committee, but the scores of people they will enlist will be those with the all-important gifts of helping and encouragement.

18

THE HOST AND HOSTESS COMMITTEE

IT WILL BE THE RESPONSIBILITY of the host and hostess committee to help enlist a host couple for each table and assign four or five couples to each host and hostess. Thursday night, before the banquet, the banquet committee chairpersons will meet with all hosts and hostesses and give each a master list of attendees. Hosts and hostesses should choose the appropriate number of guests to sit at their table, being careful to select some with whom they are not acquainted, and to call them Friday and Saturday.

By Sunday morning, the host and hostess committee will prepare posters for the banquet hall lobby containing table numbers together with the names of hosts and hostesses and their guests. These will be given to the transportation-parkers-greeters committee by Sunday morning, so that the greeters might become familiar with them and display them in the lobby of the banquet hall on Sunday afternoon. Greeters will then be able to escort banquet attendees to their assigned table.

Each table will have five or six entities, including host and hostess, with each single counted individually. The committee is to prepare the appropriate number of 5 x 8 envelopes for each table. One host and hostess, three couples, and two singles would be six entities, so the committee prepares six envelopes containing six pledge cards from the publicity committee, who will have done the printing, along with six ballpoint pens.

The host and hostess at each table will secure the six envelopes in their own handbag and *must not* distribute them to the people at their table until so directed by the speaker. Distribution will come at the conclusion of the message. I cannot overstate the importance of this. *Do not* distribute the envelopes with pledge cards and pens in advance, do not call attention to

67

them, and do not put them at individual place settings. Keep them in your possession until instructed when and how to distribute them.

19

CONDUCTING THE BANQUET

NEXT TO PRAYER, the precise and detailed manner in which you walk through the evening of the pledge banquet is the most important thing you will do. You may wish to bring in an experienced speaker to motivate your people and lead them through the filling out of the pledge cards at the climax of the banquet. There are probably three reasons that might lead you and your committee to such a decision:

1. The speaker himself would be an attraction to help draw your people to the banquet.
2. You as pastor are less than comfortable in leading the people through the pledge time.
3. There is someone very experienced at fund-raising with whom you are comfortable.

A word of caution: *Do not let one person bring the message and another lead the people through the filling out of the pledge cards.* That's like courting your fiancée for a year, coming up to the proposal, having her say yes, and inviting someone else to kiss her.

You will need to seek the Lord in the choice of speaker. Whoever brings the message, this chapter discusses the steps that you or a guest speaker *must follow meticulously* through the banquet message and pledging time.

Banquet guests have been involved, informed, and inspired. They are coming in a happy mood with receptive hearts, ready to pledge. I cannot overemphasize the importance of not allowing any surprises to be sprung upon them. They need to know they are coming for the purpose of filling out a pledge card.

The good news is that God's people have a heart to give, and they know it costs money to carry on the ministries of their church. Aren't the Lord's people wonderful? They are the only folks in the world who will joyously and willingly attend an event, knowing full well the only purpose of that event is to ask for their money.

As people enter the banquet room, the greeters warmly welcome them and escort them to their preassigned table. The host and hostess are at their table thirty minutes early, prayed up, full of the Spirit, dressed nicely, in a good mood, and carrying envelopes containing pledge cards and pens. Let me reemphasize the importance of keeping these items out of sight and of not distributing the pledge cards until told to do so by the speaker at the appropriate time, which will come after the dinner and message.

It is critical to understand the importance of timing during the banquet. Speed of service is top priority. It is crucial that the people not serve themselves. While allowing for late seating for those who arrive after serving has begun, do begin promptly at the announced hour.

If the pastor is to be the speaker, he or she should not speak until the message. If not, the pastor may preside or simply introduce the speaker, though others should participate. The master of ceremonies for the evening should be an upbeat person experienced at the task and coached in the importance of brevity.

The chairperson of the campaign may preside, but it may be best to have someone else preside and save him or her for another part of the program. At 6:00 P.M., the master of ceremonies should give a brief welcome, no more than thirty to forty-five seconds, offering brief comments about the importance, purpose, and joy of the evening. Someone should then lead in prayer—perhaps a child, young person, or aged and respected saint of God. Serving should begin immediately, with background music provided during the serving as well as the meal.

You can save time by having dessert already on the table, along with the salad. While the people are not to be hurried, waiters and waitresses should begin removing used plates as the people finish. They need not wait until everyone has finished eating and remove them all at once. The attendees will be more comfortable in resting an elbow on the table during the message as well as having room to fill out their pledge cards if plates and most other items have been removed.

From the time of the conclusion of the opening prayer to the beginning of the program, the ideal time is forty-five to fifty minutes, but one hour is clearly maximum. The program should be very short. Congregational singing is probably not appropriate at a banquet. The program should consist of a word of appreciation by the campaign chairman with an encouraging word to the people about their pledging. The chairperson should also simply recognize the committees and have them stand at one time for applause. Every individual committee member should not be named, nor should the people stand as individual committees, but they should stand collectively at the conclusion of the introduction.

Following a word of appreciation, encouragement, and collective committee introduction by the general chairman, only three other things should happen, and those with great rapidity. First, a highly respected member should give a three- to four- minute testimony. This should not be an announcement of the amount the person is going to pledge, but an expression of support for the program and joy in being a part of funding it. Second, someone should offer a brief introduction of the speaker; followed, third, by one special musical number.

At this point, the speaker rises to the podium. This servant of God must be well prepared, prayed up, and filled with the Spirit and must understand clearly the purpose and process of the evening. It is always good to begin with a word of humor to relax the listeners.

Then the speaker should say, "Before we continue, I know you've been sitting a long time, so why don't we stand and relax a minute." After the people stand and chat for a few seconds, the speaker should say, "Now, why don't you feel free to turn your chairs around so you can conveniently look this way. Thank you. You may be seated."

The speaker's brief opening remarks should express humility and appreciation for the joy of participating in the event as well as his great support for the project. He should assure everyone that he has studied the building program and believes wholeheartedly that it is, indeed, the correct next step for the congregation to take.

It is then important to get right to the point and bring a brief message, with three or four or five things that the people need to keep in mind as they pledge.

Later chapters offer sample sermon ideas which the pastor may use on Sunday mornings leading up to the event or which also may be used at the banquet. You have purchased this book, so feel free to use the sermons, mixing them together, changing them, and adding to them in any manner you please without credit to the author.

It may be very important at some point to work information about the whole concept of pledging and borrowing into your remarks. In regard to pledging, remind the people that while some may say "I don't believe in pledging," in fact, we pledge every day. Every time you sign a check, you pledge to the payee that you have money in the bank to cover the amount. Every time you use a credit card, whether it be a Sears, Visa, Texaco, or another, you're pledging to pay the amount for which you have signed. If you have served in the military, obtained a driver's license, joined a church or civic club, signed a lease or a note at the bank, or stood at the marriage altar, you have pledged. Yes, we believe in pledging, and we practice it. But urge your congregation to keep clearly in focus that we pledge to that which we believe to be important. And if we pledge to all these lesser things, how much greater the joy and privilege of pledging to our Lord and his church.

Concerning borrowing, it may be well to state that since there will likely be some interim and long-term borrowing along the way, we need to remind ourselves that, contrary to the teachings of some, borrowing is not a sin. The biblical prohibition is not against borrowing; it is against borrowing and not paying what you owe. And, of course, there is scriptural judgment pronounced on those lenders who charge usury or exorbitant interest. It is a shame that some have extrapolated Paul's words, "Do not owe anyone anything," into a prohibition against debt. He admonishes us in Romans 13:7–8, "Pay your obligations to everyone: taxes to those you owe taxes, tolls to those you owe tolls, respect to those you owe respect, and honor to those you owe honor. Do not owe anyone anything, except to love one another, for the one who loves another has fulfilled the law."

Clearly, the apostle is saying this: We ought to pay what we owe. We owe kindness, loyalty, honor, truthfulness, and service to others, and we dare not come behind in paying those obvious obligations. Do not be lacking in what you owe any person in any aspect.

Our Lord himself said in Matthew 5:42, "Give to the one who asks you, and don't turn away from the one who wants to borrow from you." On what possible basis can one harmonize Jesus' admonition to lend to those in need with the absurd teaching that lending is a sin? Perhaps one of the clearest teachings to be found on the subject is Deuteronomy 28:9, "The LORD will establish you as his holy people, as he promised you on oath, if you keep the commands of the LORD your God and walk in his ways." Verse 12 states, "The LORD will open the heavens, the storehouse of his bounty, to send rain on your land in season and to bless all the work of your hands. You will lend to many nations but will borrow from none." Verse 15 continues, "However, if you do not obey the LORD your God and do not carefully follow all his commands and decrees I am giving you today, all these curses will come upon you and overtake you." Verse 43 says, "The alien who lives among you will rise above you higher and higher, but you will sink lower and lower." And, finally, verse 44 tells us, "He will lend to you, but you will not lend to him. He will be the head, but you will be the tail."

Clearly our Lord is telling Israel, "If you disobey me, a part of the natural result is that you will be poor, and will borrow from others." Conversely, he makes it clear that if they honor and obey him, they will be blessed and will actually have enough money to lend to others.

It may not be appropriate to deal briefly with this issue at the banquet, but it will be in the minds of some people, and in the right time and place, you should address this matter. But it is certainly appropriate to deal with the legitimacy of pledging if it has not been adequately addressed in another context with the congregation, perhaps on an earlier Sunday morning.

The message should be to the point, well illustrated, and not too long. It is important to reach just the right moment of excitement and anticipation when you lead the people through the pledging process. If you have passed your prime point thirty or forty minutes earlier in the evening, you will not reach your goal. Remember the old axiom, "Leave them wanting more." Don't give them an evening so crammed full that they are exhausted. Lead up with exciting anticipation to just the right point, and then pledge, rejoice, and go home.

The entire event from invocation to benediction should be two hours, with two hours and fifteen minutes being the maximum. The time elapsing from the opening welcome to the beginning of the message should be fifty minutes to an hour, leaving thirty minutes for the message and twenty minutes to distribute the pledge cards, fill them out, bring them to the front, pray over them, and have the benediction.

The process which follows the message is critical. Pastor, *either follow this method yourself if you bring the message or see that your guest speaker does.* The message should conclude with a heart-moving illustration.

At this point, I'm going to ask you just to listen in on the pledging process of a banquet, which I have written in my own words exactly as I have spoken them at many such banquets. Had you been at my most recent banquet, this is what you would have heard following the message:

"May we bow our heads. For the next two or three minutes, I'm going to ask you to be very, very still. I know that can seem like a long time when we are in total silence, but it will be the two or three most important minutes of the campaign. Many of you have come tonight with a predetermined amount of money you intend to pledge. You have probably arrived at that number on the basis of human calculation. You may have said, 'My income is $4,000 a month, my house payment is $800, my car payment is $375, my tithe is $400, et cetera,' and you have, by human rationale and logic, determined that you can pledge an additional $50 or $100 per month. Such human logic pledges only from our apparent resources.

"Unfortunately, it allows room for no miraculous or supernatural provision from God. And it certainly allows for no faith. It is a mere human calculation which anyone can make—a Buddhist, an agnostic, an unbeliever, anyone. We don't know the future. Perhaps you're going to get a raise. Perhaps someone will leave you some money, or perhaps there will be illness and job loss. But the fact is, we don't know how much we can actually give. But God knows.

"And so tonight I'm going to ask you to give not simply by *reason* but by *revelation* as well. I want you to open your mind to God and ask him to speak to you. Only he knows the future; only he holds tomorrow. He knows how much he can trust you with, and he will specifically lead you. Luke 6:38 promises, 'Give, and it will be given to you; a good measure, pressed down, shaken together, and running over will be poured into your lap.'

"The eyes of the Lord are searching to and fro looking for those he may bless. God really wants to bless you. He wants to use you as a conduit through which he can bless your church and your world. God will let a lot of money pass through your hands if not much of it sticks to your fingers.

"Tonight, we only ask that you honestly ask him how much he wants to pass through your fingers for this campaign. And this I promise you, if you can honestly leave tonight and say, 'I heard from God, and I was obedient. I did precisely what the Lord wanted me to do,' then whether that amount is $500 or $500,000, God will be honored, and we will be pleased.

"So at this time, I want you to ask God to clear your mind of anything and everything else, cleanse it in the blood of Christ, make it sensitive to his voice, and spend two minutes in silence and listening.

"Don't expect to hear the voice of God in your ear; you will hear it much more clearly in your soul. There will come a thought, an idea, an amount, not in an audible voice, but in an impression, a deep, settled sense of an amount of money you should pledge. That thought will keep recurring. God will make it clear, and you will know. How do you know when you're in love? You just know. How do you know when you're cold or hungry? You just know. How will you know when he speaks to your heart? You will know. You will know.

"Now, with each head bowed and each eye closed, for two minutes, let's listen for the heart of God."

It is best that there be no background music at this time. At the end of two minutes, return to the microphone and say, "In Jesus' name we pray, amen.

"At this time, I'm going to ask every couple to turn to each other, in a whispered conversation, and privately discuss what the Lord has said to each of you. Now, let me say this, and I'm not trying to be humorous. If you should find that you're each thinking about a different amount, I want to encourage you to pledge the larger amount. Stretch out a bit, reach up higher, and trust the Lord."

After allowing another minute or two for discussion, continue, "At this time, I'm going to ask the host and hostess at each table to take their envelopes containing a pen and pledge card and distribute one to each person or each couple at their table. Please take your time as you fill them out together. Do be careful, please, to make clear the total amount of the three-year pledge, though you may have written a monthly amount to be multiplied by 36 or a weekly amount to be multiplied by 156."

Watch the people and try to determine when they are through, usually in about five minutes. Then say, "All right. Is there anyone who is not finished? We'll wait just another minute." The host and hostess are, of course, setting the example, filling out their own pledge card in front of those at their table simultaneously.

"Is there anyone else who is not finished? At this time, being certain that your card is completely filled out, will you please place it back in your envelope and return it to your table hostess." (Wait thirty seconds.) "Host and hostess, will one of you now rise and bring the envelopes to the chest before me." (The host and hostess committee will have purchased an inexpensive chest from a variety store, or will have made a decorated pasteboard box, that will have been placed on a table in front of the podium at the beginning of the evening.)

Give them plenty of time and then say, "Are there any other cards at all? All right. Now that we have them all in the chest and our host and hostess have returned to their seats, I'm going to ask the chairperson of deacons (or elders or presbyters or trustees) to come forward, along with the building committee chair, campaign committee chair, finance committee chair, and pastor."

When they gather at the front, continue. "Ladies and gentlemen, I would like to ask you to kneel, and to reach forward, placing your hands on this chest filled with pledge cards. If there are too many, some can simply place their hands on the shoulders of those before them." Then lead the people in prayer:

Father in heaven, we thank you tonight for the faithful response of this precious congregation of men and women. We pray for the cards, for the amount of money pledged on each, and for the tender, responsive persons who have obediently and faithfully pledged the money they represent. Some have stretched much higher tonight than they can reach. They have done so obediently in faith, trusting you. I pray you will bless them. I pray you will abundantly provide over and above what they ever dreamed they could do. May they be faithful and consistent to recognize your hand of provision and be obedient and faithful servants in giving it as you provide it.

And, Father, I pray for the building committee and leaders of this church. I pray you will give them wisdom in the administration of these funds. Help them make the right decisions, that every dollar shall be used to the glory of God. And then, Father, we ask you tonight that you will translate each gift into souls for the kingdom. Save kids, get young people off the streets and into the church. Get teenagers out of the gangs and into Sunday school. Get young adults out of the clubs and into the kingdom.

By your leadership, we have planned this building program. By your provision, we trust you for the resources, and by your grace, O God, we implore you for the mighty anointing of your Spirit on thousands and thousands of lives who shall be touched through the ministries provided in this brick and mortar. To that end, we give you praise, glory, and thanksgiving. In Jesus' name, amen.

"Thank you. You may return to your seats.

"I cannot tell you what a joy it has been to be with you tonight and to be a part of this program with your wonderful pastor. I believe in you and look forward to seeing what God is going to do with you through the months and years to come." (It is important to emphasize that at no time during the entire campaign or evening have you ever suggested that it might be possible to pledge any other time but tonight.)

Conclude the banquet in this way: "It may be that there are still a few who could not bring themselves to pledge tonight, you really haven't come to grips with it or strengthened your faith to that point, or who honestly feel you have not heard from God and do not yet know his will in the amount to pledge. You may wish to take your card home or receive another at church next Sunday. Two weeks from today in the morning services, we will include those cards, the cards you have mailed in or brought to church in person, in the final announced total. We're going to keep it a secret for the next two weeks, but I'll be praying for each of you every day.

"Some of our faithful folks could not be here tonight, and we'll be sending them a cassette tape of tonight's message and a pledge card so they, along with you, can be a part of the total. Remember, the pledge card you have signed is not a legally binding document. It is a good-faith expression between you and the Lord which will help the church to plan for its future.

"You will be in my prayers, and it will be a joy to watch your church grow. It's great to be brothers and sisters in Christ in the kingdom of God. Pray for us as we pray for you through the years, that together we might be a part of answering the prayer of Jesus' heart, 'Thy will be done, and thy kingdom come on earth.' Thank you very much."

Now, turn the service back over to the pastor for closing remarks and prayer.

Immediately, the tally committee moves into high gear to quickly and confidentially total the pledge amounts, and the follow-up committee moves into action to send letters with pledge cards and cassette tapes to the non-pledges and nonattendees.

20

THE TALLY COMMITTEE

THE FINANCE COMMITTEE CHAIRPERSON should also chair the tally committee, but let new people participate in the counting. Depending on the number of pledge cards you anticipate, enlist from five to fifteen individuals, each with calculators. It is important that no individual tally person tells his or her total to any of the others. You do not want them getting together and pooling their own totals to determine one grand total. That is a secret known only to the finance committee/tally committee chairperson, campaign chairperson, and pastor, and it must be closely guarded. A part of the excitement that brings the follow-up efforts to a positive and profitable conclusion is the promise that the total will be announced on Sunday morning two weeks from the day of the campaign. All the pastor should do during those two weeks is to grin a lot and say, "Keep those cards and letters coming in, folks. It's looking good."

Each counter brings an individual total from ten to fifty cards to the tally committee chairperson. The chairperson adds up the separate totals, swears to secrecy, and gives that amount only to the campaign chairperson and pastor. The tally committee should meet the following Sunday night and total any additional cards that have come in through the week, plus those that came in during the Sunday morning service on the Sunday after the pledge banquet, and add them to the total.

The second Sunday after the banquet should be "Victory Sunday," the day in which the pastor announces the grand total. The second Sunday after the banquet, Victory Sunday, the tally committee should meet in the pastor's office or the financial office with all additional cards that come in through the offering plates during the morning service or services and be prepared to hand the pastor a grand total to announce to the congregation. This Victory Sunday/Announcement Sunday is the Sunday morning two weeks after the banquet.

In the event of only one morning service, the pastor simply announces the total at the conclusion of the service. If there are two morning services, the best announcement procedure is as follows: The tally committee collects additional pledge cards, plus those which have been coming in during the past two weeks, and adds them to the running total between the services.

In the second service, the committee collects cards early in the service and quickly adds them to the total as well. This offers three different ways to announce the grand total: The early congregation can be invited to stay in, standing around the walls and hearing the final total, during the early part of the second service and then be dismissed to Sunday school or to go home. They can be asked to come back after Sunday school, which meets during the second morning service, arriving early enough to hear the final total announced at the end of the second service. Another possibility is to announce the total in the evening service.

If the latter procedure is chosen, don't prolong the agony until the end of the evening service. Announce it at the first. Let the campaign committee chairman give the report and praise God by bragging on the people and commending them for the great job they've done, encouraging them to be faithful, with the assurance that yet others will pledge and even more will come in.

21

THE FOLLOW-UP COMMITTEE

THERE ARE THREE IMPORTANT PHASES to the follow-up process:

1. The letters that go out on Monday after the banquet
2. The pledge cards that are distributed in the services the two following Sundays
3. Quarterly or semiannual follow-up minicampaigns for new members throughout the duration of the three-year pledging period.

First, the letters: Of exceedingly high importance for this committee is the first thing they will do, which is to make a cassette recording of the message brought at the banquet. The night of the banquet, make a clear, sharp, perhaps even professional recording of the speaker's message, *including his closing appeal* as he leads the people to fill out the pledge cards and return them to the front and pray over them. Be prepared to have the tapes reproduced immediately Monday morning. Services are readily available to duplicate them at a reasonable cost. Also, make a professional quality videotape of the message and the entire pledging process for the follow-up dinners.

Suppose you have 500 giving entities in your church. Address an envelope to each one of them during week one before pledge Sunday. Insert a pledge card and the following letter from the pastor and campaign chairperson in each one. On Monday morning, the follow-up committee will meet and get a list of the names of everyone who pledged at the banquet. Throw away those envelopes and put the letter and a copy of the cassette tape in every remaining envelope. Those are the people who did not attend or attended but did not pledge. Get that letter with the cassette and pledge card in the mail immediately. It is critical that the people have it by Tuesday at best, or Wednesday at the latest.

Make sure you have anticipated the amount of postage it will take to cover the letter, the pledge card, and the cassette. Do not even think about sending them any way but first class. The pastor and chairperson will have written the letter, which the follow-up committee will print and enclose in each envelope. It will read something like this:

Dear Bill and Mary:

We want you to have an opportunity to hear the wonderful message that was brought by so-and-so (if it's the pastor's message, only the chairman signs the letter) at last Sunday night's pledge banquet in our great "Together We Build" campaign. We had a marvelous time and wish you could have been there.

I know how much you must have wanted to attend, and we want you to know that you can still be a part of the total to be announced a week from Sunday, (A.M. or P.M.), the (day) of (month). And, Bill and Mary, we need you. God has been so good, and we are so close. I know we are not going to stop without going over the top, but we need for you to be a part of the final total.

Will you please be kind enough to listen to the tape that you might catch the excitement and feel the spirit of the evening we enjoyed last Sunday night? Then please pray about your pledge card, fill it out as God leads you, and send it back, so we might include your pledge as a part of the total amount to be announced. Please mail in your card or turn it in upside down in the offering plate next Sunday. We love you, and thank God for your support and prayers.

Sincerely,
Pastor John

It is critical that this letter and envelopes be ready in advance. Yes, you will waste a few dollars by preaddressing envelopes, but it will save you a lot of time. You need not stamp them or insert the letter and the cassette until you have thrown away the envelopes of those who have already pledged. Hand deliver them to the nearest post office with a prayer and a commitment to God.

Another important responsibility for the follow-up committee is to see that the backs of the pews are stuffed with pledge cards the Sunday after the pledge banquet and before Victory Sunday, the day of the announcement. The committee should restock them between multiple services, as well as before the evening service both Sundays. Remind the pastor to make an appeal in each of those two Sunday services, saying, "If you were not able to be at the banquet or for any other reason have not yet pledged, you may turn in your pledge cards today. You may have received one in the mail, or you can find one in the back of the pew if you have forgotten yours." Again, remind the pastor to do that well in advance of the offering time so the people will have time to fill them out, and remind them again to place them in the plates just before the offertory prayer.

A final important responsibility of the follow-up committee happens over the three-year duration of the pledges. I suggest a miniature version of the campaign twice a year for the following three years. Don't approach the issue too quickly with new members. Let them settle in for a few months and then conduct a smaller version of the campaign for a couple of months, inviting them to a dinner, perhaps in someone's home, with an opportunity to hear a couple of testimonies, one by a person who really believes in the building program and one by an individual who has already been blessed by pledging and giving.

A musical number and a viewing of the sermon and closing appeal from the videotape should follow, whereupon the pastor prayerfully leads them through the pledging process as outlined in chapter 19. Make sure to play the tape on a good sharp system. Also, make sure that hosts and hostesses have pledge card packets and that they distribute them only when instructed to do so, as was done at the original banquet.

The committee should continue a limited amount of publicity to encourage the church throughout the three-year period of the pledges. Occasionally use testimonies of those who have been greatly blessed for the manner in which they obediently pledged in faith, and publish weekly reports in the church paper about the running total. You may or may not choose to write a follow-up letter thanking the people for their pledge, specifying the amount.

It is important not to leave the fruit lying on the ground. Follow-up is crucial. The follow-up committee must do it quickly and must take the responsibility very, very seriously.

22

THINGS NOT TO DO

AS MENTIONED EARLIER, circumstances allowed me to help rewrite what, to my knowledge, was the first such campaign plan ever written in 1966. Since that time, I have preached at countless banquets and advised many churches, and have kept my eye pretty closely on the professional church fund-raising industry. I earlier stated that most professionals do a very good job. Further, I have never found any I believe to be crooked, high-pressure, illegitimate, or insincere in any way. I do, however, have some strong convictions about three or four aspects of most of their programs, which I believe are mistakes. Some are not only less than effective but actually counterproductive. Let's look at a few.

The most prominent error is leading a church to believe they can pledge more than they actually can, resulting in a great deal of discouragement and disappointment. At this moment, I am talking with a church with which I became involved after the fact. The fund-raiser told them they could pledge the full $8 million amount they wanted and advised them to "go for broke" in their building campaign and "do it all at once." In fact, they pledged between $3.8 and $3.9 million. Following the formula I outlined earlier, I would have told that church their maximum figure was $4 million, not $8 million. In two successful campaigns last year, I advised First Baptist Church of Spring, Texas, that they could pledge $2.7 million, and they pledged $2.8. Additionally, I told First Church of the Nazarene in Houston, Texas, that they could pledge $750,000, and they pledged $820,000.

A professional fund-raiser must walk the fine line between integrity and enthusiasm when it comes to selling a program. Better to err on the conservative side and leave the people with a good taste in their mouth, ready to do a second program three or four years down the line. My aforementioned formula is usually very much in the ballpark.

Sometimes the overenthusiastic fund-raiser sets as many as three or four goals before the church—a "Victory Goal" of $600,000, a "Glory Goal" of $750,000, a "Hallelujah Goal" of a million or more, and so on. Trust me. While you may know that even $600,000 itself is an optimistic goal, the congregation gets locked into thinking about that highest goal. Three cheers for positive thinking, but churches just don't pledge $20,000 and $30,000 per person attending the banquet in this or any other program. Three thousand dollars is the norm per attending family entity in a blue-collar church, with $6,000 to $8,000 if a church is mostly professional, and very rarely as much as $10,0000 to $12,000—and then only if extraordinary factors are present.

A second oft-used ingredient which I discourage is the "advance pledge dinner." The idea supposedly is to "get a feel for what the people are going to do" in order to see how the campaign is going. *I find no logic whatsoever in this.* To the contrary, I believe it to be counterproductive for two reasons: First, whether by design or accident, the word gets out about the amount pledged, and while some of the people may be challenged and stimulated by this figure, many more will do their own calculations and think, "Yes, but they're the most financially successful people in the church. They should have given more because they are more financially blessed. If that's all they pledged, I am justified in giving less."

The second problem with the advance pledge dinner is that the persons involved have not had the full benefit of the campaign. They've not heard all the sermons. They have not had the same amount of time for the Spirit of God to deal with them as those who wait until the banquet. And most important of all, they have not had the benefit of the climactic event. They've not heard the message, they've not been together with the people in a setting prepared just for this purpose, and they've not been a part of the group in a key time of waiting quietly before God. It's like asking a woman to marry you when you haven't finished the courtship process.

The fund-raiser often justifies this advance dinner on the basis that, "Well, these are just tentative pledges." Who wants to know if they may or may not get married? Let's go through the courtship before we pop the question! You don't want anything tentative whatsoever in your program. It is to be *definite, certain, and sure.* A smaller event also negates the importance of the corporate prayer time at the banquet in which we ask God to speak to us all, because it increases the likelihood that the advance pledgers will be locked in at a lower amount and less likely to hear from God about a possible higher amount.

I strongly feel it is a mistake to have an advance gifts dinner. Let me urge that if you insist on doing so and announcing the results, that you announce a corporate total rather than having individual testimonies, which brings me to another thing to avoid in your program.

Often, regardless of whether they are members of the advanced gifts group or not, someone asks these individuals to give personal testimonies about specific amounts of money they are going to pledge. Supposedly the theory behind this is to "get the people thinking up." Hearing numbers of $10,000 and $25,000 supposedly sets the pace for each person to think, *Gee, I need to be thinking about giving more than $500 or $1,000.* I strongly recommend against the public personal testimony about a specific amount. The reasons are obvious:

- The person doing so is very uncomfortable.
- The people are always uncomfortable hearing it.
- It tends to be more guilt giving than inspirational giving.
- It may be counterproductive in that the people begin to analyze. It may sound good for Joe Smith to announce $25,000, but if I know Joe Smith to be worth a million or two, I may start figuring proportionally backwards and decide that I'm off the hook for only $600 or $800.
- It is virtually impossible to give such a testimony without some personal aggrandizement. There's a thin line here between who's getting the glory: The testifier, or the one for whose glory he is supposedly giving the money?

Jesus says in Matthew 6:3, "But when you give to the poor, don't let your left hand know what your right hand is doing."

Yet another mistake, perhaps the biggest, is to bypass the banquet or bypass the opportunity to pledge at the banquet and go straight to the homes to ask for the pledges. There are three reasons this approach is not effective:

1. No one will have the inspiration in the one-on-one meeting in the home that they could have had at a well-planned and anointed banquet. When the people of God get together, wonderful things happen. There's power in the body of Christ. The whole church being inspired, all the people hearing the message, the entire body praying

together and filling out the cards together creates an *eternal moment* in which God meets his people. In a home, that simply doesn't happen, and, to that degree, the campaign loses potential to ignite an entire church with its enthusiasm and momentum.

2. Most people hate the high-pressure tactic of going into a home, looking in another's eyes, handing a prospect a pledge card, and asking for a commitment. It's quite a different issue to have gone into the homes to take the brochure, pray with the people, answer questions, find their spiritual needs and report them, and get a reservation for the banquet.

3. Even worse, not only don't the home visitors like to ask people to fill out the cards in their homes, but the persons they visit don't like it either. To be put "on the spot" by the Spirit of God at the banquet is one thing. To be put on the spot by another person in one's own home is quite another. And there's really no comfortable way to do one-on-one, in-home solicitations.

I recently tried to help pick up the pieces of a church whose program has been unsuccessful because they had bypassed pledging at the banquet and had gone into the homes. The leadership couldn't twist enough arms to recruit even a third of the number of people needed to go into members' homes, and the few who did respond were asked to make far too many calls. The people in the homes felt they were being put on the spot, and everything about the campaign was miserably unsuccessful.

The will of God is often an unfolding revelation. Things change. The apostle Paul said, "I have become all things to all people, so that I may by all means save some" (1 Cor. 9:22b). The message must never change, but the methods must be ever changing. Too many of these programs have not been allowed to evolve and develop. Every year we look at every program in our church and ask, "Is there a better way?"

Fund-raising techniques, like programs, are ever evolving, too. For example, I am currently helping to raise $25 million to build a new Christian high school in Houston. We are working with eight churches and already have approximately four thousand names in our database. We're going to approach these people in a series of in-home dinner parties with ten to twenty couples at each. In this particular case, we think that will be best. I hope you will be open to some of the evolving ideas that I have learned in my continuing consultations with churches in their capital campaigns.

Unrealistic, overly optimistic goals, advance gifts, public testimonies that name specific amounts, and asking for pledges in the homes ought to be yesterday's news. How excited I am for you as you begin this journey! I've developed the plan over more than thirty-five years, and it works. Pray down the power of God on it, and get ready for a thrill. You and your church are going to be blessed.

23

COUNTDOWN CALENDAR

MONTH FOUR: START-UP

1. Church votes to enter capital campaign.
2. Pastor enlists general campaign chairperson.
3. General chairperson and pastor unveil calendar plan.
4. Pastor and general campaign chairperson enlist all committee chairs.
5. Committee chairs, pastor, and general chairperson enlist committee members.
6. Pastor and general chairperson train all committees in the presence of one another.
7. Church conducts first of three prayer meetings for campaign.
8. Weekly church newspaper begins weekly information notices to congregation.

MONTH THREE: PRAYER, PUBLICITY, AND PROMOTION

1. All committees begin to function and report to weekly steering committee meetings.
2. Additional prayer meetings are organized and scheduled.
3. Testimonials are scheduled throughout campaign.
4. Brochure design begins.
5. Banquet meeting date, time, and place are scheduled.
6. Pastor begins three-part series on stewardship at end of month.
7. Publicity committee increases campaign visibility through banners, letters, and newsletter.

MONTH TWO: PRAYER, PUBLICITY, AND PROMOTION

1. Pastor continues stewardship series.
2. Testimonies in Sunday services begin.
3. All printed materials are completed and distributed to appropriate committees.
4. Sunday school lessons begin.

MONTH ONE: THE FINAL COUNTDOWN (FOUR-THREE-TWO-ONE . . . PLEDGE BANQUET)

Week Four

1. Letters go out from pastor about invitation teams, assuring them of no in-home solicitation.
2. Church holds second major prayer meeting.
3. Testimonies in adult Sunday school departments begin.
4. Telephone committee calls entire adult membership.
5. Pastor begins three-part motivational series.

Week Three

1. All committees create final checklist.
2. All committees participate in special prayer meeting.
3. Invitation teams visit the church family with brochures and ask for banquet reservations.

Week Two

1. Invitation committee makes repeat visits on those members not home in week three.

Week One

1. Prayer chain begins around the clock.
2. Telephone committee follows up for the second time.
3. On Wednesday committee begins calling people never contacted at home or who did not make promise to attend banquet.
4. Transportation-parking-greeters committee call all who have requested special assistance for banquet.
5. Saturday morning before Sunday evening banquet, pastor leads third major prayer meeting around the altar at the church.

6. On banquet Sunday morning, pastor or general chairman makes final appeal from pulpit for banquet reservations.

7. Committee takes reservation cards from offering plate and makes final count and reservations.

SUNDAY NIGHT PLEDGE BANQUET

After the Banquet

1. Follow-up committee sends pastoral letter with cassette tape and pledge card to nonattendees and/or nonpledgers.

2. For the next two weeks, the tally committee collects pledge cards from people not at the banquet.

3. Second Sunday after banquet, tally committee meets in pastor's office with additional cards that have come in during the morning services, and then they hand the pastor the final tally.

4. Pastor announces total to the congregation.

5. Pastor announces that there will be a follow-up once a year for new members.

24

SPECIAL FORMS

Child Care Reservation

_____
_____
_____
_____

Name: _____
Address: _____
Phone: _____

(return to appropriate committee)

Children's Party

Number: _____

Ages: _____

Name: _____
Address: _____
Phone: _____

(return to appropriate committee)

Youth Party

Number: _____

Ages: _____

Name: _____
Address: _____
Phone: _____

(return to appropriate committee)

Spiritual Needs & Prayer Requests

_____
_____
_____
_____

Name: _____
Address: _____
Phone: _____

Special Transportation Needs

_____
_____
_____
_____

Name: _____
Address: _____
Phone: _____

(return to appropriate committee)

Banquet Reservation

Number Attending _____

_____
_____
_____

Name: _____
Address: _____
Phone: _____

(return to appropriate committee)

Emergency Contact Form

My child, _____, has my permission to participate in the festivities planned for the evening's entertainment appropriate to his or her age.

Cellular contact: _____ Phone:_____

Emergency contact: These people will be notified if neither parent can be contacted in case of emergency:

Name:_____ Phone: _____ Relation: _____

Physician's Name: _____

Physician's Phone: _____

I hereby authorize Houston's First Church of the Nazarene, or designated representative, to give consent for any and all necessary medical care in which parent cannot be reached.

Parent's Signature: _____ Date: _____

Notes:
(Any special requirements, individual concerns, or limitations)

25

STEWARDSHIP SERMON 1

"THE ONE MINUTE MANAGER"

Then God said, "Let Us make man in Our image, according to Our likeness; and let them rule over the fish of the sea and over the birds of the sky and over the cattle and over all the earth, and over every creeping thing that creeps on the earth." . . . Then the LORD God took the man and put him into the garden of Eden to cultivate it and keep it.
(Gen. 1:26, 2:15 NASB)

KEN BLANCHARD'S BOOK *The One Minute Manager* has been read by millions. God's book is about the original One Minute Manager. Genesis makes it clear that the purpose of God for his creation is to manage his world—to be in charge—to oversee his creation. James 4:14 says, "You don't even know what tomorrow will bring—what your life will be! For you are a bit of smoke that appears for a little while, then vanishes." Second Peter 3:8: "Dear friends, don't let this one thing escape you: with the Lord one day is like a thousand years, and a thousand years like one day." As God counts time, we are here only about a minute out of eternity. Our purpose? To manage the things of God. The biblical word is "stewardship." Today's modern word is "managerialship." We are, indeed, one minute managers.

The number one theme in the Bible is salvation. Number two is stewardship, or management. In thirty-two of the thirty-five parables, Jesus taught about being good managers or stewards. The dictionary defines a *steward* as "one who manages the affairs or assets of another."

(1) *All creation is God's because He created it.* Good managers remember that God is the owner and we are the managers. It is not ours. He created it and it is his. We think we create, but we indeed do not. We only mix

and match and alter things God has created. Whether it is a piece of furniture, a car, or a house, all are God's. We speak of "my boat," "my car," "my house," but regardless of what possessive pronoun we use, all belongs to him who created all things.

(2) *Everything is God's because he sustains all things.* Newton's second law of thermodynamics teaches that "everything left to itself declines." Contrary to the claims of the evolutionist, nothing in fact evolves—everything devolves. A Ford pickup left in a field for a century will not evolve into a Cadillac. It will turn to rust, disintegrate, and go back to the earth from whence it came. Who upholds life? God does. By him all things were not only created; they are held together. And he does so, Peter says, "by the word of his mouth." What causes the planets to stay in their orbits and the stars to remain in their sockets? What is the power of gravitation and the essence of centrifugal force? It is Jesus Christ. Colossians 1:16–17 explains this fact completely. "All things have been created through Him and for Him . . . and by Him all things hold together." God didn't walk away from his creation. He made it and sustains it by the word of his mouth.

(3) *Being a good manager gives God glory.* The Shorter Catechism answers the question, "What is the purpose of man?" in this way: "The purpose of man is to glorify God and enjoy him forever." In fact, the purpose of man is to be a good one-minute manager. And doing *that* gives God glory.

(4) *Being a good manager gives God pleasure.* All parents know what it means to give their children money with which to purchase a Christmas present for Mommy and Daddy. The parent takes great pleasure in seeing the child receive pleasure from giving the parents the gift on Christmas morning, even though it is the parent's money that bought the gift. Just so, God who is the owner takes pleasure in the pleasure his children receive in managing the possessions he gives them.

(5) *Being a good manager applies to all of life.* You will notice that this stewardship sermon has not even mentioned the words *money* or *tithe*. Good one-minute managers manage everything: their environment, their time, their minds, their bodies, their influence, their talents, every part of their lives. Tithing their income is only an indicator of their acknowledgment of God's ownership of all things and their temporary stewardship of them.

(6) *Being a good one-minute manager is the key to life.* Jesus said it another way in Matthew 6:33: "But seek first the kingdom of God and His righteousness, and all these things will be provided for you." Managerialship

is about lordship—it keeps clearly in focus the center of my life. God owns it all, and I have the privilege of managing just a bit for a very short minute.

(7) *Just as good managers get more to manage, poor managers lose what they have. Good managers are promoted to manage even more.* Poor managers are dismissed. In the parable of the talents, Jesus commended the good steward who made a good profit and condemned the man who managed his money into no profit whatsoever.

After two years in a row failing to advance to the Super Bowl, on virtually the last play of the game, Bud Adams fired the popular Houston Oilers coach, Bum Phillips. The sportswriters were incensed and the city was up in arms. What right did Bud Adams have to fire Bum Phillips when he had come so close two years in a row? That's simple. He was the owner.

(8) *No owner shares everything with his manager.* God always holds back something for himself in the arena in which man earns his living, so that man never forgets that God is the owner and he, just the manager. God gave man six days to labor and said the seventh is to be spent worshiping him. In the garden, Adam could eat of every tree but one. God said, "Don't touch that tree—that is my tree. In so doing, you learn the principal that you are just the manager—and I the owner."

In Canaan, God told Israel to let the land rest every seventh year. Six years the land could be cultivated, planted, and harvested. But God said, "Rest the land in the seventh year. That year belongs to me." For 490 years, Israel disobeyed, and owed God seventy years of rested land. Then the Babylonians carried them into captivity. And for how long? That's right—seventy years. The prophet says, "And then had the land its rest." God always holds back something for himself so that we never forget he is the owner and we the manager.

The owner of a large grocery store agreed to allow a neighboring church to use the store's parking lot for overflow church traffic on Sunday mornings. "However, pastor," he said, "one Sunday morning a year you will find a chain across the parking lot. That," he said to the puzzled pastor, "is so the church never forgets the parking lot belongs to the grocery store and not to the church." The "Tithe Is the Lord's" sign across the parking lot of our lives is our reminder and our acknowledgment that he is the owner and we are the temporary stewards—the one-minute managers of everything in God's world.

STEWARDSHIP SERMON 2
"A PASTOR'S TESTIMONY"*

Give to everyone who asks of you, and whoever takes away what is yours, do not demand it back. And just as you want people to treat you, treat them in the same way. And if you love those who love you, what credit is that to you? For even sinners love those who love them. And if you do good to those who do good to you, what credit is that to you? For even sinners do the same. And if you lend to those from whom you expect to receive, what credit is that to you? Even sinners lend to sinners, in order to receive back the same amount. But love your enemies, and do good, and lend, expecting nothing in return; and your reward will be great, and you will be sons of the Most High; for He Himself is kind to ungrateful and evil men. Be merciful, just as your Father is merciful. And do not judge and you will not be judged; and do not condemn, and you will not be condemned; pardon, and you will be pardoned. Give, and it will be given to you; good measure, pressed down, shaken together, running over, they will pour into your lap. For by your standard of measure it will be measured to you in return.

(Luke 6:30–38 NASB)

I DO NOT GIVE TITHES AND OFFERINGS because I am a pastor; I do so because I love the Lord and long to please him with my obedience. I have been a giving person since I first came to know him. Before I was a pastor, I was a tither. Before I learned to preach, I learned to give. This morning's message is a personal testimony. I want to share with you as your pastor, friend to friend, the simple testimony of some things I have learned through the ministry of my own stewardship across many years of giving to the Lord.

(1) *Giving is the easiest thing I do.* It is the most natural and joyous part of my Christian experience. I love the Lord, and I love to give. I first began

to give out of obedience. The Bible told me to do it, and I obeyed. I will not tell you that there were not times that it was hard to give. But those times have long since gone. Now it is easy. I love it. I cannot conceive of not doing it. Jesus tells us that "it is more blessed to give than to receive." Today I believe that—not simply because he said it but because I have experienced it.

John Bisagno tells a story of preaching in Nigeria. One afternoon he and a party of four were rowed by twelve young African oarsmen two hours upstream to a tiny village that had never seen a Caucasian face and had never heard the name of Jesus. He preached the gospel in simplicity, and villagers, including the king, believed the story of Christ and received him into their hearts. There was weeping and there was gladness. "As we stepped back into the boat," Dr. Bisagno said, "I received the largest love offering of my life. The king handed us a stalk of bananas and two live chickens. No one had told him to give. He had heard no sermon nor studied any lesson on stewardship. The most natural thing from his heart of gratitude was to give." I can honestly say that giving is the most natural part of my life. It is like breathing air and loving my family. I cannot imagine life without it.

(2) *The real motivation is love.* There are other encouragements but only one worthy motive. Some give from obedience. And well we should. Some give from fear. And I admit that I do not want to risk what I may lose if I am disobedient. Some give in order to receive, and it is true that we do receive when we give. But these should not be our primary motive. The real motive is love. A popular bumper sticker said, "If You Love Jesus, Honk." I say, anybody can honk. If you love Jesus, *tithe.*

(3) *Tithing is giving back to God what is already his.* Leviticus 27:30 says these beautiful words about the tithe: "It is holy to the LORD."

Let's look at the meaning of this assertion. The word *tithe* means "a tenth part," or 10 percent. I encourage you to give it off the top before taxes. Far better too much than too little. The verb *is* represents the present tense of the verb infinitive "to be," indicating possession or ownership. *Holy* means "set apart or sacred." The Bible calls only six things holy, and one is the tithe. You may be wearing the Lord's tithe, driving the Lord's tithe, or living in the Lord's tithe, but it is still his, and he attaches a special blessing to the person who lives by that.

(4) *Giving is always to the Lord.* The Bible knows nothing of giving to building funds, mission causes, televangelists, or even church budgets; those are merely channels through which we give. Keep in focus that giving is always to the Lord. Giving is an eternal investment in that which is dearest

to the heart of God. It advances his kingdom, wins those for whom he died, and brings honor to his name. What joy is to be found in giving! Men like Kraft, LeTourneau, J. C. Penny, and others found such great blessing in giving that they gradually increased their percentage to 90 percent by the time of their deaths. Their testimonies were the same—the passion to give paralleled an increasing passion of love. Learn to keep the sweet face of Jesus always before your face as you give. Giving is always to the Lord—never primarily to the cause.

(5) *Giving is through the church.* Hear again these powerful words from the apostle in 1 Corinthians 16:1–2: "Now about the collection for the saints: you should do the same as I instructed the Galatian churches. On the first day of the week, each of you is to set something aside and save to the extent that he prospers, so that no collections will need to be made when I come."

The first day of the week is Sunday. On the first day, the New Testament church meets. That is the place and the time to bring your tithes. Malachi 3:10 refers to "the storehouse" as the place to bring tithes, and every Jew knew about this building. It was where the Jew brought grain to store and where he received his grain in times of need. The church clearly has become the New Testament storehouse. "To the extent that he prospers" is an obvious reference to percentage giving. We give in relationship to our prosperity. Tithing, or 10 percent giving, is clearly in view. The thesis is simple: bring your tithe to church on Sunday, as an act of worship and devotion. You should give to evangelistic organizations, Christian universities, Christian schools, TV ministries, and mission organizations *over and above* the tithe. Giving is always *to the Lord and through the church.*

(6) *Giving is more downright fun than you can imagine.* (Pastor, use your own stories here.) John Bisagno tells three stories about the fun of giving. "In our first year of the ministry," he writes, "we were so poor we had to pick up Coke bottles on the side of the road to buy Christmas gifts. But, we gave a tithe of those bottles to Jesus and had a wonderful Christmas." "In DeWitt, Arkansas," he continues, "God really came through in a special love offering. The people gave us about $400 in cash but filled the back seat and trunk of our car with canned goods, rice, and frozen ducks, which carried us through almost the first half of the year." He continues, "But, perhaps the best is this. In college, Jack Edmonds and I drove four hundred miles round trip every night for two weeks to conduct a youth revival that resulted in the conversion of only one small boy. Two weeks after the

revival, the issue arose in that church's business meeting that the love offering may have been too much for such meager results. Midway into the business meeting, a rugged, weather-beaten old rancher strode to the front of the congregation, took out his checkbook, and said, 'If all you people will come down here and tell me how much you gave to the love offering, I will personally give everyone of you your money back. 'Yes,' he continued, 'there was only one little boy converted—but that boy was my little boy.'"

I commend to you the ministry of tithing and the joy of giving. I have not only read about it and believed it—but have personally experienced its great blessing for all of my Christian life.

*This sermon is to be given in first person.

27

STEWARDSHIP SERMON 3
"FIVE PRINCIPLES OF PROSPERITY"

WHILE OUR HIGHEST MOTIVATION TO GIVE IS LOVE, the principle remains that when we do give, we receive. God wants to bless his children, and he has placed firmly in Scripture five principles for financial blessing.

(1) *God owns everything in this world and the world to come.* David was a great giver and loved to lead Israel to be generous. Before each time of offering, he led the people to acknowledge that everything comes from the Lord. That prayer is recorded in 1 Chronicles 29:10–13:

> So David blessed the LORD in the sight of all the assembly; and David said, "Blessed art Thou, O LORD God of Israel our father, forever and ever. Thine, O LORD, is the greatness and the power and the glory and the victory and the majesty, indeed everything that is in the heavens and the earth; Thine is the dominion, O LORD, and Thou dost exalt Thyself as head over all. Both riches and honor come from Thee, and Thou dost rule over all, and in Thy hand is power and might; and it lies in Thy hand to make great, and to strengthen everyone. Now therefore, our God, we thank Thee, and praise Thy glorious name." (NASB)

John's prologue acknowledges God's dominion even more eloquently in John 1:1–3: "In the beginning was the Word and the Word was with God, and the Word was God. He was with God in the beginning. All things were created through Him, and apart from Him not one thing was created that has been created." It is characteristic of the Greek to emphasize by restatement. Hear again verse 3: "All things were created through Him, and apart from Him not one thing was created that has been created."

Colossians 1:16–17 affirms, "Because by Him everything was created, in heaven and on earth, the visible and the invisible, whether thrones or dominions or rulers or authorities—all things have been created through Him and for Him. He is before all things, and by Him all things hold together."

Psalm 50:10 declares, "For every beast of the forest is Mine, the cattle on a thousand hills" (NASB). He owns it all—everything. We begin with the premise that under the doctrine of stewardship and possession, God owns it all.

And yet, somehow it is also true that . . .

(2) *It all belongs to his children.* What my father has is mine. The father told the elder brother, "Son, everything I have is yours." Jesus said, "All things are yours at the Father's hand. Little children, it is the Father's good pleasure to give you the kingdom." We are sons and daughters of the kingdom. We are joint heirs with Jesus Christ.

Galatians 3:13–14 says: "Christ has redeemed us from the curse of the law by becoming a curse for us, because it is written, 'Cursed is everyone who is hung on a tree.' The purpose was that the blessing of Abraham would come to the Gentiles in Christ Jesus, so that we could receive the promise of the Spirit through faith."

What powerful words—Christ died on the cross *in order that* the blessing of Abraham might come upon us! The blessing of Abraham promised four things for the Jews:

- A great land
- A great family
- The Savior
- Prosperity—"I will bless them that bless you . . ."

If God did so much for the Jews whom he arbitrarily chose, is it not reasonable that everything he did for them, he will outdo for the believer since by his sovereignty and our free will, we chose to be obedient to his choice? Everything he did for the Jew, he *outdoes* for the believer.

- Israel was given a tiny desert land; we have a land that is fairer than day.
- Abraham had a great family; we have the worldwide family of God.
- Israel was given a Savior they rejected; we have a Savior we accepted.
- If God has outdone everything for us in land, family, and Savior, does it not stand to reason that he will do even more in providing us with material blessings?

(3) *He wants it all in circulation.* Like many of you, I recoil at the caricatured "prosperity gospel" so many preach. There is a vast difference between it and the promise of a covenant New Testament material blessing. Biblical Christians do not give in order to receive. They give from love, but they know that when they give, incidental to the giving, they will be blessed. I am an heir of all things. What belongs to my Father belongs to me. For by blood, I am his child. He wants to share everything with me. God has plenty of everything. Nothing with him is in short supply. Money is not tight in the kingdom of heaven. Everything God made, he made plenty of and desires to spread around. He is a generous, giving God, whose ample provision is never in short supply. Never! At no time! To any person! In any way! Hear his promises:

- "Whatsoever you ask in my name, that will I do."
- "Whosoever will may come."
- "Everyone that thirsts; come ye to the water."
- "Eye hath not seen, ear hath not heard, nor hath it entered into the heart of man what God has prepared for them that love Him."

Our God is a God of plenty—plenty of air, water, food, grass, and love. He wants to circulate and share his plentiful gifts, and he wants us to do the same. Communism teaches, "What's yours is mine, and I'll take it." Christianity teaches, "What's mine is yours, and I'll share it."

(4) *The secret of getting is giving.* Luke 6:38 admonishes us, "Give, and it will be given to you; good measure, pressed down, shaken together, running over, they will pour into your lap. For by your standard of measure it will be measured to you in return" (NASB). If God has so much and he wants to share it, why do I have so little? The answer has never changed, and it has been in the Bible for thousands of years. Listen again. "Give *and it will be given to you.*" The secret of getting is giving. God has placed the principles of giving to receive, losing to find, releasing to keep, and dying to live not only across the pages of Scripture but throughout the entire universe. The sun is burning itself out, releasing four million tons of energy per second. But, because the sun gives, the moon receives. Its reflected light causes the ocean's tide to ebb and flow. Job said, "He has placed boundaries upon the ocean." Without these boundaries, huge tidal waves would destroy the majority of life on earth.

The sun gives its light, and the grass can grow. The animals eat the grass. Their rotted carcasses fertilize the trees. The trees spend their lives creating oxygen without which man cannot live. All around us there is a giving cycle. All of life and all of creation give to get, in order to give to get, so it can give again. The Dead Sea is dead because it receives but does not give. Jesus taught us that as we give, others will return back to us good measure, shaken together, pressed down, and running over, and over, and over again.

Peter boasted to Jesus that he had left so much to follow him. Jesus said that everyone who had done so would receive a hundredfold *in this life*—not in heaven, *in this life!* Selfish, stingy, tight, faithless people never tap the treasure of their Father. What a pity we have so much but access so little! Most have never cashed a divine check or clipped a single heavenly coupon. What a tragedy that we live from payday to payday and only dream of things we will never have. Pray that God will give you a giving heart, and start practicing exuberant giving. God loves a reckless, joyful, even hilarious giver, and his giving to you will be in measure as you give to him and to others.

(5) *We are to give, not out of our apparent resources, but from God's actual resources.* Unfortunately, we list our income alongside our debts and say, "I have no resources from which to give," but God does. How then does one trigger the showers of heaven and tap the Father's endless provision? By faith! We give what we *cannot* afford. We pledge what we *cannot* see how we can pay. Faith moves the hand of God and brings showers of blessings from the Father's hand. Put aside that budget for a moment and ask the Lord what he would have you to pledge and to give. When he speaks to your heart, respond in faith. Without faith, it is impossible to please God. With it you will please him, and he will be pleased to bless you.

28

MOTIVATIONAL SERMON 1
"WE HAVE COME THIS FAR BY FAITH"

Now faith is the assurance of things hoped for, the conviction of things not seen. For by it the men of old gained approval. By faith we understand that the worlds were prepared by the word of God, so that what is seen was not made out of things which are visible. By faith Abel offered to God a better sacrifice than Cain, through which he obtained the testimony that he was righteous, God testifying about his gifts, and through faith, though he is dead, he still speaks. By faith Enoch was taken up so that he should not see death; and he was not found because God took him up; for he obtained the witness that before his being taken up he was pleasing to God. And without faith it is impossible to please Him, for he who comes to God must believe that He is, and that He is a rewarder of those who seek Him. By faith Noah, being warned by God about things not yet seen, in reverence prepared an ark for the salvation of his household, by which he condemned the world, and became an heir of the righteousness which is according to faith. By faith, Abraham, when he was called, obeyed by going out to a place which he was to receive for an inheritance; and he went out, not knowing where he was going. By faith he lived as an alien in the land of promise, as in a foreign land, dwelling in tents with Isaac and Jacob, fellow-heirs of the same promise; for he was looking for the city which has foundations, whose architect and builder is God. By faith even Sarah herself received ability to conceive, even beyond the proper time of life, since she considered Him faithful who had promised; therefore, also, there was born of one man, and him as good as dead at that, as many descendants AS THE STARS OF HEAVEN IN NUMBER, AND INNUMERABLE AS THE SAND WHICH IS BY THE SEASHORE. All these died in faith, without receiving the promises, but having seen them and having welcomed them from a distance, and having confessed that they were strangers and exiles on the earth. For those who say such things make it clear that they are seeking a country of their own. And indeed if they had been thinking of that country from which they went out, they would have had opportunity to return. But as it is, they desire a better country, that is a heavenly one. Therefore God is not ashamed to be called their

God; for He has prepared a city for them. By faith Abraham, when he was tested, offered up Isaac; and he who had received the promises was offering up his only begotten son; it was he to whom it was said, "IN ISAAC YOUR SEED SHALL BE CALLED." He considered that God is able to raise men even from the dead; from which he also received him back as a type. By faith Isaac blessed Jacob and Esau, even regarding things to come. By faith Jacob, as he was dying, blessed each of the sons of Joseph, and worshiped, leaning on the top of his staff. By faith Joseph, when he was dying, made mention of the exodus of the sons of Israel, and gave orders concerning his bones. By faith Moses, when he was born, was hidden for three months by his parents, because they saw he was a beautiful child; and they were not afraid of the king's edict. By faith Moses, when he had grown up, refused to be called the son of Pharaoh's daughter; choosing rather to endure ill-treatment with the people of God, than to enjoy the passing pleasures of sin; considering the reproach of Christ greater riches than the treasures of Egypt; for he was looking to the reward. By faith he left Egypt, not fearing the wrath of the king; for he endured, as seeing Him who is unseen. By faith he kept the Passover and the sprinkling of the blood, so that he who destroyed the first-born might not touch them. By faith they passed through the Red Sea as though they were passing through dry land; and the Egyptians, when they attempted it, were drowned. By faith the walls of Jericho fell down, after they had been encircled for seven days. By faith Rahab the harlot did not perish along with those who were disobedient, after she had welcomed the spies in peace. And what more shall I say? For time will fail me if I tell of Gideon, Barak, Samson, Jephthah, of David and Samuel and the prophets, who by faith conquered kingdoms, performed acts of righteousness, obtained promises, shut the mouths of lions, quenched the power of fire, escaped the edge of the sword, from weakness were made strong, became mighty in war, put foreign armies to flight. Women received back their dead by resurrection; and others were tortured, not accepting their release, in order that they might obtain a better resurrection; and others experienced mockings and scourgings, yes, also chains and imprisonment. They were stoned, they were sawn in two, they were tempted, they were put to death with the sword, they went about in sheepskins, in goatskins, being destitute, afflicted, ill-treated (men of whom the world was not worthy), wandering in deserts and mountains and caves and holes in the ground. (Heb. 11:1–38 NASB)

(Dr. Bisagno preached this sermon in March 1984. Please adapt it for your church.)

OUR RELIGION IS CALLED THE CHRISTIAN FAITH, and for good reason. We come this morning for the 143d time, in the 143-year history of this church, to recommit ourselves to yet another year of financially undergirding the work of the Lord and the body of Christ through this special fellowship, our beloved First Baptist Church.

It is a day we do not back into, nor for which we apologize. It is one we proudly step up to the line and support. It is a day our membership looks forward to. With great gladness, we are willing to say that for what God has done for us, we give gratitude and willingly commit to make it possible to continue.

Many of you are new members of our church. I can imagine that someone who has never been here before might see all these facilities, our programs, our mission outreach, our television ministry, and all the things that we are trying to do in the name of Christ . . . and suppose that someone waved a magic wand and it all just came into existence. But such, as you know, is not the case. We have decided this year to make the theme of our annual stewardship subscription program "We've Come This Far by Faith," as we pledge again for the work of the Lord for yet another year. But, we want you to know something of how we got here and what went into this, and where we think the Lord wants us to go. And so I want to present six things to you this morning about "We've Come This Far by Faith."

(1) For one thing, I want you to know that *we have come a long, long way*. I read again this week some of the history of this church and the years of struggle and difficulty here: of hurricanes and depressions, inflation and financial problems, world wars, and times of divisions and disunity. And yet, when we suffer much, we grow much. This church has given millions of dollars, and sent hundreds of her sons and daughters into full-time Christian service as her ministries and influence have for well over one hundred years extended around the world.

Our modern history has been a blessed one, as well. In the last fifteen years, you have given over $100 million to the work of our Lord Jesus Christ. Thousands of persons have come to Christ. During the past few years, we have received more than a thousand new members per year, and the Lord continues to bless.

Dr. Peter Wagner of Fuller Seminary is one of the world's eminent missiologists. His particular area of expertise is statistics in the modern growth of Christianity. He tells us that the church is growing three times faster then the birth rate in Brazil. He has also determined that 56,000 persons a day worldwide are coming to Christ. Dr. Wagner led a study in 1982 to determine the strongest churches in the world based on stewardship, Sunday school attendance, and total membership. Dr. Wagner has written us to report that by those criteria, the First Baptist Church of Houston is the eleventh largest church in all the world. The Lord has been very good to us. We have indeed come a long, long way.

(2) In spite of our progress, the second thing I want to say to you is this: *We have a very, very long way to go.* Before we pat ourselves on the back, let's point out that we are in a battle to build the kingdom of God. Dear friends, as the second oldest Baptist church in Texas, and as the First Baptist Church of Houston, we have an extremely large responsibility to the kingdom of God right here in our own city.

I am increasingly impressed with the necessity to touch our town for Christ in a real way and broaden our local mission efforts. Jesus said to begin in Jerusalem, and Houston is our Jerusalem. Let me tell you how well we are *not* doing.

During the last decade, one million persons have moved into Harris County. We have 265 Southern Baptist churches, and would you believe that 90 percent of them are the same size or smaller than they were ten years ago? Only 10 percent of our churches are growing. We have to do a better job. I believe the responsibility of the "First Church" of any denomination is extremely important as it gives leadership and inspiration in its own community, and I am convinced that we must make an increased effort in mission outreach in this city. For one thing, I would hope that First Baptist Church could be instrumental in beginning and sponsoring at least twenty-five new missions that will become churches in the Houston area in the next decade, because if in 1994 we are at least *twice* as strong as we are now, we will still be farther behind in reaching this city in 1994 than we are in 1984. We have come a long way, but if we think we have won our last soul, dreamed our last dream, given our last dollar, prayed our last prayer, and made our last sacrifice, then we need to think again. We give God glory for our success and his blessing upon us, but I want to underscore that we still have a very long way to go. We must press the battle to the gates of hell and never, never let up until Jesus Christ comes from glory.

(3) *We have come this far together.* I want to emphasize the word *together* and what it means for us as the people of God to be one in Christ. I believe the strongest, most important single factor in the life of this church is the unity of the people of God doing what we do together. We have a debt of about $7 million. Now that is very little in comparison to our budget and the $60 million valuation of our property and buildings. But if a lending firm lends money to a church, it is at once the most secure and the riskiest loan the lender can make. In fact, any member of this church can move his mem-

bership to another church next Sunday and completely walk away from his part of that obligation. But the president of Northwestern Bank told me only recently that in his many years of banking, he has made around $30 million worth of loans that were church-related to the people of God and has never had one default, because God's people have something special in the way of commitment to one another and to the cause of Christ. In the New Testament, the people of God lived with unbelievable opposition and oppression, and yet the early church greatly multiplied. Historians say the reason was a tremendous sense of *koinonia*, fellowship, unity, and oneness. They truly believed that what happened to *all of them* corporately was more important to *each of them* than what happened to *any of them*. I want to say that again. They believed that what happened to all of them was more important to each of them than what happened to any of them. There was a tremendous spirit that would sacrifice homes and jobs and land or anything for the cause of Christ and his kingdom. And that same spirit has brought this church through 143 years to where it is today. We Have Come This Far by Faith and we have come together.

(4) *We have come this far by tithing.* You know the Lord did a wonderful, wonderful thing when he created the tithe—the 10 percent—because whether you are a pauper, whether you have a dollar to your name, whether you live on a pension, whether you make a small salary, or whether you earn a million dollars a year, the fact is that everybody has a fair share in giving the tithe.

Three years ago, we went into a program called Two by Two, and hundreds of our people signed a two-year pledge card that promised, "I will either begin tithing, or if I am tithing, I will double my tithe." Today, three years later, that program is over, and yet the offerings haven't dropped. Why? Because our people have experienced the blessing of giving at an accelerated rate, and most have never even considered going back. If you are tithing, I challenge you to keep doing so and perhaps even make a pledge to increase it 1 or 2 percent this year. And, if you are not tithing, let each at least begin to come up to the standard.

The tithe is the Lord's. I want you to hear that. Out of every dollar you receive in your check, only 90 percent, according to the Book of Books (and it is not the Book of the Month, but the Book of the Ages), is the Lord's. The prophet asked, "Will a man rob God? How do we rob you?" The answer from heaven is, "In tithes and offerings" (Mal. 3:8). These are strong words! You would by far be better off personally, financially, and eternally to take a gun and rob a bank than to rob God of his tithe. The tithe is *holy* unto the Lord. We have come a long way because the people of God have equally sacrificed and prayed and honored God with what is his.

(5) The fifth thing I want to say to you is this. *We have come this far by pledging.* Let's talk about pledging for a moment. From time to time, persons say, "I don't believe in pledging, and I don't want to sign a card. I will give, but I will not pledge." Well, may I say to you that after thirty-two years in the Lord's work full-time, I have run across maybe one or two persons who give generously but won't sign a pledge card. When people say they don't believe in pledging, what they really mean is, "I don't believe in tithing," because we are usually willing to pledge to what we believe in. We stand at an altar and pledge to be faithful to a wife. We sign a note at the bank and pledge to pay it back. Many of you have gasoline cards, American Express cards, and other credit cards. When you signed for those cards, you pledged to pay the creditor! You pledge allegiance to the United States of America; you get a driver's license and sign your name and pledge to obey the laws of your state. Oh, we believe in pledging all right, and we pledge every day. But we pledge to what we believe in, and if we really believe in the Lord's Word and his commandments and his church and in tithing as the Bible tells us, we will pledge to tithe. Well now, we have come a long way. We have a long way to go. We have come this far together, and we have come this far by tithing and by pledging.

(6) The last thing I want to say is this: *We have come this far by faith.* This congregation has never been able reasonably or logically to deduce how we could do anything we have done; we just do it because God says to. We do it because the need is there. We do it because we must. The story has been told through the years about how the church was nearly lost in the 1920s, and four of our men went to New Orleans to plead with a mortgage company not to foreclose. From 9:00 in the morning until noon they met. At noon the bankers said, "We are going to come back at one o'clock and sign the foreclosure papers." Our men went to their hotel room and said, "Lord, we have done all we can," and they prayed. They called home to the church members and requested them to pray. They went back at one o'clock to the meeting, and the bankers told them, "We have changed our minds. We are not going to foreclose on your church."

In 1960, when the church was in a great financial need, Mrs. K. Owen White, the pastor's wife, put her wedding ring in the offering plate. We found that ring in the church safe about two years ago and, as you know, sent it back to her. The people of God have always come through. I remember that after we tried to get on television for two years, I went to our deacons when the opportunity finally came and said, "We have the opportunity to go on two stations at once in Houston." They asked, "What will it cost?" I answered, "Not much—only $6,000 a week." The church's entire budget was only $6,000 a week! We could not conceivably do it at all. But we just did it. We signed up as an act of faith, and twelve years later we are still on— and we are on other stations, as well. We have never been a dollar short or a week late. I don't think Moses stood at the Red Sea scratching his head and thinking, *If those waters would ever split, I'd get caught in them.* I don't think he had a choice! He didn't have any options! He had to go forward! Without faith it is impossible to please God! I don't know how 90 percent goes farther than 100 percent, but it does. I challenge you to be 100 percent faithful in this and to step up to the line and express your faith in the Lord's work for another year and as long as Jesus tarries.

Let me tell you one other story. In 1972, this church was doing very well—our buildings were nearly full. It was obvious that the future was bright, and we realized we had to relocate or stagnate because we couldn't buy any more property downtown. We offered the Sakowitz Department Store a half million dollars for air rights, just for the privilege of building on top of the store. We couldn't get any land, and without it we couldn't grow. We were stuck, so the congregation voted to move. The architect drew the plans and estimated it would cost $3.2 million—a lot more money in 1972 than it is in 1984. We held a stewardship campaign and we worked and struggled and wept and prayed and sacrificed and prayed some more and signed our pledge cards and opened them, and the people had pledged $3.2 million. We rejoiced and breathed a sigh of relief and thirty days later opened the bids. The lowest: $8.1 million! I went before our people and said, "It is your church, and you must make the decision, so you decide." And the people of God stood to their feet and roared their unanimous approval: "No matter what it costs, we must go forward." They pledged that money, and they gave that money, and you and I twelve years later are sitting here looking around at perhaps the most wonderful church facility in all the world because the people of God were willing to make the sacrifice.

We have come a long way. We have a long way to go. Let us trust the Lord and let us remember . . . .

We Have Come This Far by Faith!

29

MOTIVATIONAL SERMON 2

"WE ARE DRIVEN"

"For the love of Christ controls us, having concluded this, that one died for all, therefore all died; and He died for all, that they who live should no longer live for themselves, but for Him who died and rose again on their behalf." (2 Cor. 5:14–15 NASB)

CHRISTIANS ARE A DRIVEN PEOPLE. We are constrained, pressed, beside ourselves, outside ourselves, and beyond ourselves with passion to spread the gospel. In earlier days, the Nissan Motor Company, then the Datsun Company, had an excellent slogan: "We Are Driven." The Greek word in our text translated "controls" means "compelled with an explosive force." We, too, are a driven people.

Too many churches have no sense of conquest and no sense of urgency. But churches that are winning the day are churches with an insatiable desire for souls. We must cross the next river, forge the next stream, climb the next mountain, and reach the unreachable star for the heartbeat of God's conquering, winning people.

Jesus was a driven man. When Peter would dissuade him from Jerusalem, he said, "I must go there and die." Haven't we enough members, enough building, enough staff? What are the forces within that drive us to want more? There are three that I want to share today.

(1) *We are driven to the end of ourselves by the love of Christ.* His love constrains us; his love impels us to give our fortunes, our lives, and our all for him. A real man died on a real cross. And those who know him—truly know him—never get over it.

Hyman Appleman, a Hebrew Christian, was at one time the most widely heard evangelist in the world next to Billy Sunday and Billy Graham. His

Jewish mother never heard him preach. In fact, she had a mock funeral and buried him following his conversion to Christ. Near her death, she came to Hyman's home to plead with him to renounce his faith in Christ and to return to the practice of Judaism. Her son kissed her good-bye as she stepped on the platform of the train, tears streaming down her face. Doctor Appleman said he came very close to turning his back on the cross. "Slowly," he said, "over the horizon of that train above the head of my weeping mother, behind the outstretched arms of the woman who nearly gave her life to give me mine, there arose the vision of a hill . . . and on a hill, an old rugged cross." Hyman turned his back on his mother and walked away to give his life to preaching the gospel. The love of Christ constrains us and we are driven to the end of ourselves by that love.

(2) *We are driven to the ends of the earth by the Great Commission.* Acts 1:8 records our Lord's last words: "But you will receive power when the Holy Spirit has come upon you, and you will be My witnesses in Jerusalem, and in all Judea and Samaria, and to the ends of the earth." Jesus listed Judea to emphasize witnessing to all the world's great religions, and he singled out Samaria as a symbol for the world's various ethnic groups. The "ends of the earth" means all men and women for all time. By the most conservative estimates, well over one billion persons and perhaps as many as two billion have never even heard the name of Jesus. It is said that in Japan alone it takes all the Protestant denominations and mission agencies combined to win one-twentieth of one day's birth rate per year to Christ. This means that for every person we reach in Japan, over seven thousand perish without the Savior.

The once proud republic we call "America, Columbia, the gem of the ocean, the home of the free and the brave" is teetering on the brink of decay. In some places in the world, three Muslim mosques are begun for every new church. On my last trip to Russia, the back one-third of the plane was filled with Mormon missionaries. Africa is dying of AIDS. It is reported that as many as forty-thousand a week are perishing. How can we stand still? How can we be satisfied with the status quo in a world in which millions are rushing headlong into eternity without the Lord? The church that is standing still is backing up. Until Jesus comes, we must buy more land, build more buildings, start more classes, hire more staff, give more money, and win more lost souls to our Lord.

(3) *We are driven to the end of time by the coming of Christ.* Our Lord did not create the world and abandon it. He created humanity to give him

glory. And one day every knee shall bow and every tongue confess that Jesus is Lord to the glory of the Father. Our Lord will come to judge the world and set up his earthly kingdom, a showcase of how life could have been from the beginning under the lordship of Christ in every heart. The Bible is filled with hundreds of signs indicating the time of his return. In Matthew 24, Jesus names many of them and then declares, as recorded in verse 33, "In the same way, when you see all these things, know that He is near—at the door!" Be very careful to note that he says "when you see *all* these things," not just "some" or "many" of these things. Many of these signs have happened from time to time throughout the centuries. But Jesus said there would come a time when all these things would be happening at once. And that time is now! No signs remain to be fulfilled, no prophecies must be completed, before Jesus returns for his bride, the church. The season of his coming is now.

The urgency of the church to fulfill the Great Commission has never been greater. Hebrews reminds us we are surrounded by "a large cloud of witnesses." The saints of heaven are a witness to us of the faithfulness of Christ—the seriousness of his Word—the urgency of his commands. O church, arise! It is time to sacrifice, to pledge, to give, to go, to build, and to win! His cross constrains us; his Commission sends us; his coming stirs us. We are a driven people.

30

MOTIVATIONAL SERMON 3
"WINNING THE DAY"

IN THE MID 1970S, completely unrelated and even unknown to each other, Edwin Young and Adrian Rogers did independent studies of the top twenty-five largest and fastest growing evangelistic churches in America. Some were in the north, some in the south, some met in cathedral-like sanctuaries, and some in metal buildings. The two pastors sought to determine what, if any, common factors were present in all the churches. To no one's surprise, both completed their study with precisely the same list.

(1) *They were all under strong pastoral leadership.* In each case, the two researchers reported that it did not take long to see where the power lay in these churches. Let it be clearly noted that these pastors were not dictators. Leadership must be earned and neither coerced nor demanded. The pastors were earning the right to lead, and the people were willing to grant it. Many Bible teachers have done disservice to the Book of Ephesians for the passage on the wife's submission to her husband. The passage begins by saying, "Husbands and wives are to submit themselves to each other." As a husband pours out his life in loving honor and service to his wife, she returns that honor in grace and humility. A husband doesn't demand the wife's respect in the home; he earns it. Similarly, the pastor, or undershepherd, is the earthly husband to Christ's bride, the church, and earns his congregation's love and respect.

(2) *Each was a Bible church.* The pastors were not defending the Word of God, apologizing for it, or trying to prove it. They believed it to be perfect and complete and preached it authoritatively. Strong Bible churches attract large numbers of people.

Where is security to be found? God's Word. Great churches have a high view of Scripture. Our society is hungry for authority, security, and confidence in something they can believe in. The government, the home, and the church, our three pillars of stability, are shaking. In government, the Kennedys, the Nixons, the Harts, and the Clintons disappoint us. In the home, parents desert and abandon their children, and more marriages dissolve by divorce than stay together. In the church, the Bakkers, Swaggarts, and Tiltons disillusion us. But God's Word is stable and consistent.

(3) *These churches were happy churches.* They were not stuffy and formal, and not controlled by tradition. They were bright, happy churches that had learned to sing with freedom and rejoice with exuberance.

(4) *The churches were in unity with themselves and their Lord.* They were not characterized by splits and fights, division and cliques. The unity of God's people creates his presence. Jesus prayed that his followers might be one in order that the world might believe he came from God. The unity of God's people is inseparably linked to world evangelism. When we are in harmony with one another, each in honor deferring to the other, not demanding our own way, something very special happens. The Holy Spirit flows the life of Jesus the head in heaven through his body the church on earth, creating what Scripture repeatedly calls "the body of Christ." When Jesus was on earth, he was limited to one body. How could he say, "These works that I do shall you do and greater." Because he now indwells a larger body, the church. Let our church unite around doctrinal integrity, a passion for the lost, and the lordship of Christ, and watch the people come! Where that unity exists, the presence of Christ is powerful and real. We must guard our unity as a precious and priceless treasure and maintain it at all costs.

(5) *Each church had an indomitable sense of conquest.* There was an insatiable appetite for more. Three years into my first pastorate in Oklahoma, I apologized to my church for pushing them so hard for so long to give more, build more, and win more.

The president of our Woman's Missionay Society drew me aside and said, "Pastor, don't ever do that again. Nearly twenty-five years ago, the doctors informed us that we would have twins. The boys were born and we almost never went a day without grumbling. Yes, there was joy, but there were two hospital bills, two cribs, two sets of diapers, two sets of school clothes, two cars, and two college tuitions. It never let up and it was never easy. A week before their twenty-second birthday, the boys were stricken with a mysterious illness. Within six weeks, they were dead. From that day until this, Pastor, they haven't cost us a dime."

There is nothing more expensive than a dead church. And yes, it does cost money to advance the kingdom. The water of life is free, but the pipes through which it flows are not. Onward, upward, and forward for the kingdom and for our coming Lord!

31

SUNDAY SCHOOL LESSON OUTLINE 1
"WHY SHOULD A CHRISTIAN TITHE?"

Key Verse: "Bring the whole tithe into the storehouse, so that there may be
food in My house, and test Me now in this," says the Lord of hosts,
"if I will not open for you the windows of heaven, and pour out for you a
blessing until it overflows." (Mal. 3:10 NASB)

I.   Tithing is obedience to God's plan.
   A.   It is a *personal* plan . . . "bring (you) . . ."
   B.   It is a *percentage* plan . . . "the whole tithe . . ."
   C.   It is a *practical* plan. It offers a guide for systematic giving.
   D.   It is a *priority.* It comes off the top, not from what is left over.
         Proverbs 3: "Honor the Lord from your wealth, and from the
         first of all your produce" (NASB).
   E.   It suggests a *place:* "Into the storehouse ." The storehouse is
         the forerunner of the local church. Paul told the Corinthian
         Christians to give to the Lord through the church.

II. Tithing was endorsed by Jesus.
     Matthew 23:23 NASB: "Woe to you, scribes and Pharisees, hypocrites!
     For you tithe mint and dill and cummin, and have neglected the
     weightier provisions of the law: justice and mercy and faithfulness;
     but these are the things you should have done without neglecting the
     others."

III. Tithing helps keep money in its proper perspective.
     It makes a statement that God comes first, not money. It acknowl-
     edges God's ownership of all you have. Psalm 24:1 NASB: "The earth
     is the Lord's, and all it contains, The world, and those who dwell in
     it."

118

IV. Tithing is an antidote to selfishness.

By nature, we are takers more than givers. Tithing allows us to deny ourselves and give to God. 2 Corinthians 8:1–3 NASB: "Now, brethren, we wish to make known to you the grace of God which has been given in the churches of Macedonia, that in a great ordeal of affliction their abundance of joy and their deep poverty overflowed in the wealth of their liberality. For I testify that according to their ability, and beyond their ability they gave of their own accord."

V. Tithing is the only way God has told us that we can prove him.

Is God real? Is he faithful? Try tithing and discover him. Discover that he is at work. Malachi 3:10b: "'And test Me now in this,' says the LORD of hosts."

VI. Tithing brings God's involvement into your life and finances.

Malachi 3:10 NASB: "'Bring the whole tithe into the storehouse, so that there may be food in My house, and test Me now in this,' says the LORD of hosts, 'if I will not open to you the windows of heaven, and pour out for you a blessing until it overflows.'"

VII. Tithing brings immediate blessings from God.

"'. . . if I will not open up for you the windows of heaven, And pour out for you a blessing until there is no more need.'"

VIII. Tithing brings the supernatural protection of God.

Malachi 3:11 NASB: "'Then I will rebuke the devourer for you, so that it may not destroy the fruits of the ground; nor will your vine in the field cast its grapes,' says the LORD of hosts."

IX. Tithing expands your faith.

You are trusting God to multiply what is left after tithing and faithfully to meet every need. Hebrews 11:6: "Now without faith it is impossible to please God." *You will never know the joy of tithing until you tithe.* The great news is you don't have to stop there.

X. Tithing is the fairest way to build the church and expand the kingdom. Both rich and poor share equitably in the work and rewards of God.

32

SUNDAY SCHOOL LESSON OUTLINE 2
"HOW DO WE HONOR GOD BY HELPING OTHERS?"

Key Verse: "Now this I say, he who sows sparingly shall also reap sparingly; and he who sows bountifully shall also reap bountifully. Let each one do just as he has purposed in his heart; not grudgingly or under compulsion; for God loves a cheerful giver."
(2 Cor. 9:6–7 NASB)

Central Truth: God desires his children to be "rivers of blessing," not reservoirs of stagnation. We build up our church family and reach the lost by giving.

Teaching Aim: At the conclusion of this lesson, participants will understand the Christian mandate to bless others. Each Christian is under God's authority to tithe with a cheerful attitude.

MOTIVATION

The principles of the Christian life are not altered by time, place, or circumstance. Christians throughout history have been givers and helpers. United together, they have sent missionaries, built hospitals, established orphanages, reunited and strengthened families, and spread the gospel.

I. Who are we to help?
A recurring New Testament theme is that we actually grow stronger by helping others (Luke 6:38). As individuals or as families, we need to reach out beyond our own interests.
A. *We should help our families.* 1 Timothy 5:8 NASB: "But if anyone does not provide for his own, and especially for those of his household, he has denied the faith, and is worse than an unbeliever."

Question: Since this is a command of God, can I include support of a parent or a child as part of my tithe?

Answer: The tithe is to be given to the local church. God promises to supply your needs after you tithe.

B.   *We should help our church.* Tithes and offerings are the sole support of our church. Not only is helping the church commanded by God; it is our privilege to join hands with other believers in helping people around the world.

II.   How are we to help through tithing in our church?
Although there are many ways to help and serve, the most regular and beneficial financial help is the tithe.

Who is to give?

Response: Every Christian (Luke 6:38; 2 Cor. 9:6–7; Mark 12:41–44)

What are we to give?

Response: A tithe of our material possessions (Mal. 3:8–10)

Where are we to give?

Response: Our church (Mal. 3:10; 1 Cor. 16:2)

How are we to give?

Response: Cheerfully (2 Cor. 9:7)

Why are we to give?

Response: Obedience (Luke 11:42), Blessing (Luke 6:38); Discipleship (Matt. 6:21)

Illustration—Tipping or Tithing?

Why do we give a waitress 15 percent in a restaurant and give God 10 percent in church? John 3:16 NASB: "For God so loved the world that He gave His one and only son." Matthew 10:8 NASB: "Freely you received, freely give."

III.   What is a biblical example of Christians helping others?

A touching example of people helping others beyond their apparent means is shared in 2 Corinthians 8:1–5 NASB: "Now, brethren, we wish to make known to you the grace of God which has been given in the churches of Macedonia, that in a great ordeal of affliction their abundance of joy and their deep poverty overflowed in the wealth of their liberality. For I testify that according to their ability, and beyond their ability they gave of their own accord, begging us with much entreaty for the favor of participation in the support of the saints, and this, not as we had expected, but they first gave themselves to the Lord and to us by the will of God."

A.   *They gave by faith and not by circumstances* (vv. 1–2). Macedonia had been wrecked by a succession of civil wars fought on their territory. Christians also were subject to persecution (1 Thess. 1:6, 2:14; Acts 16:20, 17:5). Yet even in their poverty, they wanted to give to needier believers in Judea.

B.   *They desired to give a gift of high quality* (v. 2). Paul characterizes their gift as abundant in the "wealth of their liberality." James Moffatt translates this phrase as "a flood of rich generosity." Even in their poverty they were not content to give the bare minimum.

C.   *They gave with no outside pressure* (vv. 3–4). J. B. Phillips translates verse 3: "I can guarantee that they were willing to give to the limit of their means, yes and beyond their means, without the slightest urging from me or anyone else." Christians should expect money to be discussed in the church. Finances are a part of our lives. A preacher or teacher who does not mention money is not being true to God's Word. Pressure, however, should come only from the Holy Spirit.

Illustration

Multimillionaire R. G. LeTourneau committed to give 90 percent of his income to support the Lord's work. In the epilogue to LeTourneau's autobiography, Nels E. Stjenstron of LeTourneau College offers a striking insight. "He does not view money as something to be accumulated for the satisfaction of looking at it, counting each day to check its increase, nor as a measure of man's worth. He sees it only as a means to produce the machine his mind has conceived or as a means to bring men to God."

IV.   What can each Christian do in regard to tithing?
    A.   *Acknowledge God as Lord of my personal finances.* Pray and seek godly direction for all financial decisions.
    B.   *Accept tithing as a matter of obedience to God.* Promise him:
        1.   If I'm not now tithing, I will begin a regular program of cheerfulful giving which will allow me to tithe.
        2.   If I'm already tithing, I will seek to give offerings above the tithe.
        3.   If I'm already tithing and giving offerings, I will prayerfully consider a "graduated tithe," giving a greater percentage as my income increases.
    C.   *Aspire to help others in order to be a "river of blessing."*

Illustration—The Widow's Mite

It has been calculated that if the widow's mite (Mark 12:42–44) had been deposited at the "First National Bank, Jerusalem," to draw only 4 percent interest semiannually, the fund today would total $4,800,000,000,000,000,000,000! Just in case you wondered, this figure is pronounced as four sextillion, eight hundred quintillion! How large is this figure? If you were to count from zero to one quintillion, one count per second, day and night, it would take you 32 billion years! To count to one sextillion . . . 32 trillion years! Isn't that incredible? If a bank on earth could multiply the widow's mite to such an astronomical figure, think what treasures this dedicated woman will have in heaven!

Journey to Tomorrow...
Our Next Step

J U D G E S   1 8 : 6

Houston's First
Church of the Nazarene

"...Your journey has the Lord's approval."

- Judges 18:6

Dear Church Family,

Every time I drive up to 10001 West Sam Houston Parkway North, I am amazed! Why would God choose to bless us with such a magnificent location and so much room for growth? Could it be that He trusts us and wants to use us in a mighty way to see hundreds and perhaps thousands come to know His Son, Jesus Christ, in a personal way? I think so! God's vision for our congregation is great and I believe He has given His approval to our journey.

Seventy-eight years ago, a few families living near downtown Houston caught a glimpse of God's dream for a Church of the Nazarene in their neighborhood. They invested their time, their talents, and some of their treasures to begin the church we enjoy today. No one could possibly have known the dividends their initial investment would provide. Those folks are all gone, but their sacrifices live on in the lives of people like you and me.

As we look toward the future we see the awesome opportunity God has provided for us. Two and one-half years ago we completed our first phase of construction and celebrated God's faithfulness. Who could have known how quickly we would outgrow the facility? Three sessions of Bible Study, two morning worship services, and parking on the street were not part of our plan! Thankfully, God has been with us every step of the journey.

I am so proud to be your pastor and to be making this journey with you. Your participation in the Journey to Tomorrow...Our Next Step campaign is so important. Our new education building for children and teenagers insures our ability to effectively minister to our most precious resources. The additional parking helps us send a message to the community that our congregation wants to provide a place for them to join us. Together, we can reach that goal!

Join my family in seeking God's direction for your involvement in taking this next step. Nothing will stretch you and grow your faith like sacrificial giving. Remember: we walk by faith, not by sight. God guarantees our success when we walk with Him.

Thanks for sharing God's journey with me!

Expectantly,

Keith

Pastor Keith Newman

Journey *to* Tomorrow...
OUR NEXT STEP
JUDGES 18:6

126

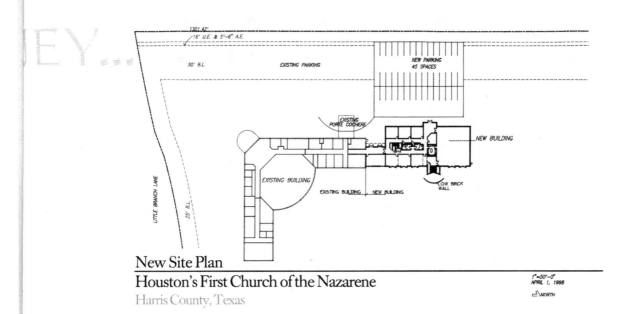

New Site Plan

Houston's First Church of the Nazarene

Harris County, Texas

1"=50'-0"
APRIL 1, 1998

NORTH

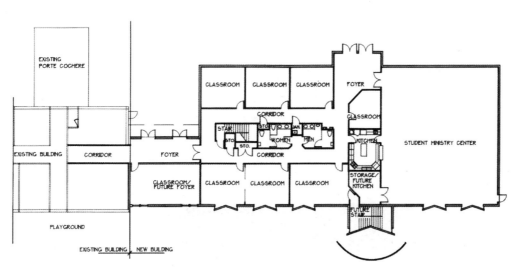

New Floor Plan

Houston's First Church of the Nazarene

Harris County, Texas

1/16"=1'-0"
APRIL 1, 1998

NORTH

You've got questions and we've got answers!

"What are we building?"

We are seeking to build a functional two-story education building designed to be most effective for children and youth ministries. The proposed plan includes completion of the two-story structure and finish work on the first floor, which will provide eight classrooms, a new kitchen, and a student ministry center. Also included is the addition of 45 new parking spaces.

"How much will this building cost?"

Our best estimate now is $750,000 for the two-story structure, finish work on the first floor, and parking. This is only an estimate. The actual figure may be different.

"How will this be paid for?"

The congregation is being challenged to make three-year financial pledges over and above their regular giving to the ongoing ministry of the church. The building will be paid for with a combination of these funds and borrowed money.

"How much in pledges do we need to receive to move forward?"

We must receive at least $600,000 in pledges to satisfy the bank's loan requirements. This figure will allow us to complete the first floor of the new building. Plans are to finish the second floor at a later date.

What happens if we pledge more than $600,000?

We believe this can happen! Pledging more than $600,000 would allow us to do several things: 1) save money in interest and retire our debt principal more quickly; 2) possibly proceed with finishing the second story which would provide even more educational space; 3) allow us to add more than the 45 parking spaces.

When will my pledge be made, and for how long?

Pledges will be made at our banquet on May 3 and are for a period of three years.

When will we be able to begin using our new building?

Construction is scheduled to begin this summer with completion in the fall of this year.

EXISTING BUILDING | NEW BUILDING

New Elevation - East

Houston's First Church of the Nazarene

Harris County, Texas

1/16"=1'-0"
APRIL 4, 1998

NORTH

"I'm excited about our new building...

"... because right now we have to meet in the Nursery on Wednesday nights.

Chelsea Updegraff–9

"...because the more space we have the more people can come to know God."

Karen Ford-Hollaway–16

"..because it gives us a place to run and play without getting in trouble."

Ashley Martinez–10

"...because it gives children and youth more room for worship."

Jessica Cork–15

"...and for the people following me who will benefit from it."

Kirt Garrison–18

"...BECAUSE THERE WILL BE MORE ROOM AND A GYM."

Rafael Flores–11

"...because we can have more and more people learning how Great Christ is in our lives."

Jared Tostado–13

Journey
to
Tomorrow...
OUR NEXT STEP

Where We're Going ... Our Goal!

Our goals are simple: $600,000 and 100% involvement! Please take a moment to look at the table below and you'll see what a difference you can make!

My Gift Makes a Difference

Weekly	Monthly	Annually	3-Year Total
5.00	21.67	260.00	780.00
8.00	34.57	416.00	1,284.00
10.00	43.33	520.00	1,560.00
15.00	65.00	780.00	2,340.00
20.00	86.67	1,040.00	3,120.00
25.00	108.33	1,300.00	3,900.00
30.00	130.00	1,560.00	4,680.00
40.00	173.33	2,080.00	6,240.00
50.00	216.67	2,600.00	7,800.00
60.00	260.00	3,120.00	9,360.00
75.00	325.00	3,900.00	11,700.00
100.00	433.33	5,200.00	15,600.00
300.00	1,299.00	15,600.00	45,800.00

Our Next Step ... Begins With You

Your First Step: Pray

Sacrificial giving usually requires us to move outside our comfort zone and stretches our faith as we give beyond our normal gifts. Please make the amount of your gift a matter of daily prayer, seeking to find what God wants you to give.

Your Second Step: Discuss

Families should take time to discuss this matter and seek God's guidance together. Children should also have a part in deciding the amount to give. This is a journey for everyone!

Your Next Step: Commit

It is vital that everyone in our church faithfully seeks God's guidance about what they should do and then express that faith in a financial and prayer commitment. This journey we're on will only become reality through the sacrificial commitments we make.

For more information, contact:
HOUSTON'S FIRST CHURCH OF THE NAZARENE
281-897-0300
P. O. BOX 41898 / HOUSTON, TEXAS 77241-1898